ROBERT
SERVICE

AMAZING STORIES

ROBERT SERVICE

The True Adventures of Yukon's Favourite Bard

ELLE ANDRA-WARNER

Heritage House Publishing Company Ltd.
heritagehouse.ca

Originally published by Altitude Publishing Canada Ltd.

Cataloguing information available from Library And Archives Canada
978-1-77203-331-1 (pbk)
978-1-77203-332-8 (epub)

Cover photograph: Yukon Archives, Gillis family fonds, 4531
Maps by Scott Manktelow

The interior of this book was produced on 100% post-consumer recycled
paper, processed chlorine free, and printed with vegetable-based inks.

Heritage House gratefully acknowledges that the land on which we
live and work is within the traditional territories of the Lkwungen
(Esquimalt and Songhees), Malahat, Pacheedaht, Scia'new, T'Sou-ke, and
W̱SÁNEĆ (Pauquachin, Tsartlip, Tsawout, Tseycum) Peoples.

We acknowledge the financial support of the Government of Canada
through the Canada Book Fund (CBF) and the Canada Council for the
Arts, and the Province of British Columbia through the British Columbia
Arts Council and the Book Publishing Tax Credit.

24 23 22 21 20   1 2 3 4 5

Printed in Canada

Contents

Foreword

ALTHOUGH I WAS only six years old when he died, his kind image is engraved on my childhood memories. He stays for me a good man, simple, sensitive, generous, passionate about the beauty of nature, and loving liberty very much. He loved to play with me and my sister when his work left him some time. His life philosophy was very simple: "Freedom is heaven, lack of it, hell." As he wrote, let us grow happiness in our inner garden, and make his motto ours: "All is well."

MADAME ANNE LONGEPÉ Granddaughter of Robert Service

Prologue

AT THE AGE of 13, Robert Service had a burning desire to be a sailor. He fantasized about being a mariner on the high seas, and spent every Saturday down at the docks admiring the ships. His parents, however, set out to defuse this passion. When they insisted he would have to stay in school for another year, he vowed to be a terrible student. And he was.

Robert made a point to arrive late to class. He ignored the lessons and drew caricatures of the teachers. When a teacher would ask him a question, he would give sassy answers to make the other students laugh. His defiant behaviour made him a thorn in the side of authority, and the boy was on the fast track to being expelled.

Then one day, a simple childhood prank on his drillmaster, Sergeant William Walker, became the final straw. A retired soldier with twenty-two years experience in the Northumberland Fusiliers, Walker was a strict disciplinarian who had no time for jokes. But Robert didn't care. When he was made master of his class's drill company for the day, he decided to have some fun. In a deep voice, he commanded his classmates to quick march, and then marched them straight into the school washrooms. Everyone laughed—everyone except Sergeant Walker.

Robert's actions merited a visit to the headmaster, who simply said to the boy, "Perhaps it might be better if you ceased coming." So, at the age of 14, Robert's formal schooling ended. His teachers predicted he would be a failure in life, but Robert Service went on to become the most successful—and likely the richest—poet of the twentieth century.

1

The Scottish
Years

PERHAPS UNCONVENTIONALITY WAS in Robert William Service's blood. He was born on January 16, 1874, in Preston, England, the eldest of ten children. His father, Robert Service Sr., was from Kilwinning, Scotland, and his mother, Sarah Emily Parker, was from a wealthy English family that owned a cotton factory. His parents defied convention by eloping in 1872, when his father was thirty-five years old and his mother was seventeen. Emily's father, James Parker, was so furious that he severed all ties with her.

The Services continued to break with tradition. When Robert William was born two years later, he was named after his father and his father's brother William, ignoring the Scottish custom of naming the first-born son after the father's father (John).

Emily did reconcile with her father shortly before his death in 1875, and she was reinstated in his will. She inherited an annual

income of two hundred pounds, prompting Robert Sr. to resign
from his job as a bank clerk and go into business for himself as a
general commission and insurance agent. He failed, and in 1878
moved the family back to the Glasgow area, settling in nearby Kilwinning, his hometown on the River Garnock. When he failed in
business again as a commission agent, Robert Sr. decided his life-
time career would be to manage the family, which he did until he
died in Canada over thirty years later.

After moving to Kilwinning, Robert's parents brought him and
his brother John Alexander to live with their 64-year-old grandfather, John Service (the town's postmaster and registrar), and their
four unmarried aunts: Jeannie, Isobella, Agnes, and Janet. Robert
never explained why he was sent to live with his grandfather, but
it may have been to ease the parenting burden on his mother, who
was expecting her fourth child. Whatever the reason, for the next
four years, Robert lived in his grandfather's home and had little
contact with his parents. His grandfather became the key influence
in his young life.

Robert had a sheltered childhood, one that included dedicated
religious activity. His aunts, donned in their black silk skirts,
would read religious writings by the fire. Their Victorian parlour
was decorated with glossy black furniture, a grandfather clock, a
bookcase of sermons, and a collection of waxed fruit under glass.
Draped on their sofas and armchair were antimacassars, and a
needlework picture of Moses in Bulrushes hung on the wall.

When Robert was six years old, his 37-year-old aunt Agnes died
of consumption. He had thought she was the loveliest of his aunts—
and the loneliest. She was often sad, and sat apart from the family.
Robert later surmised that she forced this solitude upon herself

because she didn't want to infect the others. Agnes was a poet, and on one occasion, she decided to share her work with her young nephew. "She brought out some delicately written poems," Robert recalled. "She said they were her own and I thought them beautiful."

Agnes died on November 14, 1880, and Robert visited with her the night before she passed away. She smoked her herbal cigarettes and hugged him tightly. He always remembered the "unearthly brightness of her eyes" the last time he saw her. "She was regarded as doomed; we just waited for her to die," wrote Robert years later. "I did not understand then but now I realize how stoically she awaited death who had never really known life." It was his first experience with death.

Robert's aunt Jeannie encouraged him to learn poetry and recite long, narrative poems. Mounted on a chair in the parlour, he would do readings of dramatic poems like Henry Wadsworth Longfellow's classic, *The Wreck of the Hesperus*.

Robert wasn't the only one in his family destined to be recognized in literature. His cousin, Dr. John Service, would gain literary fame with books like *The Life and Recollections of Doctor Duguid of Kilwinning* (1887) and *The Memorables of Robin Cummell* (1913). Born in Kilwinning in 1851, Dr. Service later moved to New South Wales, Australia, where he died in 1913. Robert's uncle William became a Classics master at an exclusive girls school, and his brother, Dr. Stanley Service, wrote poetry. The Service family also talked about a distant kinship with the great Scottish poet Robert Burns.

Robert's first recital of his own work took place on his sixth birthday. A special dinner had been prepared for him, including cold boiled ham, cookies, cakes, and scones. When his grandfather was about to say grace, Robert blurted out: "Please, Grandpapa, can I say grace this time?" And then, before anyone answered, he began:

> God bless the cakes and bless the jam;
> Bless the cheese and the cold boiled ham;
> Bless the scones Aunt Jeannie makes,
> And save us all from belly-aches, Amen.

Everyone in the room went silent. Suddenly, Robert was afraid he would be punished for his boldness, but his fear was short-lived. His family was delighted, and praised his cleverness—they talked about his grace for years.

Robert lived with his grandfather and aunts until he was nine years old. His aunts wanted to adopt him, but his mother was adamant in her refusal and, in 1883, brought him to their family home in Hillhead, just outside of Glasgow. Four years later, his grandfather died at the age of seventy-six.

Now back with his family, Robert reacquainted himself with his siblings and settled into his new surroundings. For a while, he attended Church Street School along with future notables like David Bone (who became a master mariner and novelist) and Sir John Rennie (who became the governor of Mauritius). A quick wit and voracious reader, Robert was a free spirit who couldn't help but flout convention. After he was expelled from school at the age of fourteen, he worked for a time in a shipping office, and then asked his father to help him find work in a bank.

Robert Service c. 1905. LAC PA-110158

The Banking Years

Thanks to his father, Robert began his banking career with the Commercial Bank of Scotland in the summer of 1888. For the next eight years, he worked as a bank apprentice, earning twenty pounds a year. During that time, Robert became passionate about poetry, carrying around books by Tennyson and Browning, and studying verse-makers such as Thackeray and Tom Hood. He even read while he walked.

Inspired, he began writing verses and sending them out to publishers. In his autobiography, titled *Ploughman of the Moon*, he wrote that his first published verses were in Scottish newspapers like *Ching Ching's Own, Scottish Nights, People's Friend*, and the *Quiz*, a Glasgow weekly paper. Among these verses were *The Song of the Social Failure, It Must Be Done*, and *Shun Not the Strife*.

But Robert was young, and his interests changed quickly and dramatically. One day, he announced to his friends that he had given up poetry forever to be an athlete, playing cricket and rugby (he was quite a good player). When his interest in sports waned, he was lured into the glamorous world of dance halls and theatre. He trained to be an actor, taking elocution lessons to strengthen his ability to give recitations. Soon he was performing at church-hall concerts and landing small walk-on parts in plays. Then, at the age of eighteen, he got his big break in show business: a small but important role in an upcoming amateur production of *Rob Roy*. But what could have been the start of new theatrical career ended in disaster.

Robert was playing the son of Rob Roy, and his lines were short and simple. When cued, he was to rush onstage to the woman playing his mother and tell her that Rob Roy had been captured.

Then she would hug him, and his part would be over. Simple yet effective. But it didn't work out that way.

One night, while waiting for his cue, Robert had a few drinks at the theatre's adjoined bar. Some of his castmates came in and told him that the actress playing his mother was displeased with his drinking and had vowed to strike his backside when he came on the stage. To protect him, his friends jokingly turned Robert's kilt around, putting the sporran in the back. When the call came for his scene, Robert, unaware his kilt was turned around, rushed onto the stage and tripped, falling right into the actress's arms. With the audience watching, she fought him furiously, angry at the alcohol smell on his breath. It was a chaotic scene, and Robert made an early exit off the stage.

His next focus became furthering his education. In 1882, he attended a literature course at the University of Glasgow and wrote an essay on the character of Ophelia from Shakespeare's *Hamlet*. Robert wasn't very flattering in his analysis of Ophelia, referring to her as a "bit of a slut." He was confident the essay would earn him a 90 percent mark, and was shocked when it was given only 23 percent. The teacher called the essay an "obscene bit of work, unworthy of a student in this class." Robert was furious and challenged the teacher to step outside for a fistfight to settle the matter. The lecturer declined. Then, when the teacher threatened to expel him, Robert left school and never returned. Academia was not where he belonged.

The world of politics beckoned him next, giving him a new cause to promote. Robert's political interest began when he read a pamphlet titled *Merrie England*, written by Robert Blatchford, editor of a socialist weekly called *The Clarion*. The pamphlet, first published in 1893, was a collection of Blatchford's columns about the working conditions of poor people. Blatchford promoted socialism as "the hope of the world," and encouraged socialists to teach others about the movement. He tied socialism to "fellowship of life," and launched Clarion Cycling Clubs across England, combining the pleasure of cycling with the propaganda of socialism. (Eventually, two million copies of *Merrie England* were sold worldwide.)

So intrigued was 19-year-old Robert by Blatchford's message that he became an instant socialist. He was so passionate about spreading the word on the ills of social injustice that he became a street-corner orator, championing socialism to the crowds. Enthusiastically, he attended socialist meetings and read socialist literature.

But Robert began to lose interest when he found that socialists didn't welcome him into their ranks; to them, he was one of the people they ranted against. Besides, he really didn't like meeting others who were working for the same political cause, commenting later, "I have always found that my own ideas antagonize me when held by others."

Fate then led Robert's reading in a new direction—one that would ignite the first sparks of wanderlust and eventually bring him to Canada. He discovered travel writing, and books by literary wanderers such as Stevenson, Kipling, Barrow, and Thoreau.

George Barrow's *Lavengro* introduced Robert to the "gift of vagrancy," and led him to question the wisdom of a banking career. Did he really want a 40-year future of deskwork and tellers' cages? Morley Roberts's *A Western Avenue* also awakened "the spirit of vagabondage" in Robert. Now barely twenty years old, he made a life-altering decision: he would go to America and become a hobo.

While Robert was able to imagine countless exciting adventures in America, the reality was that he was an overweight banker still living with his parents. His brother Peter, who had become physically fit while working on a farm, even called him a "little fat bank clerk." Determined to lose weight, Robert took up weight-lifting, went on long walks every day, and adopted a fresh outlook on life.

He also developed a plan: as soon as he got enough money, he would quit the bank and be a farmer. When Peter suggested he move to Canada, Robert visited the Canadian emigration office to find out more. After doing some research, he became an authority on the country.

He pictured himself as a cattle rancher on the Canadian prairies, riding broncos, and roping steers. The rugged romanticism of a cowboy life was calling him. He bought a big hunting knife and an air pistol, and for hours would practise the fast gun draw. Though anxious to start his adventure, he still lacked the money.

Then fate intervened again. The bank increased his salary from twenty to seventy pounds, giving him more money to save for his Canadian journey. They also transferred him to another branch and gave him a reference letter testifying to his intelligence, willingness, and industry.

On March 31, 1896, Robert took on the challenge of adventure and resigned from the bank. He was twnety-two years old and told his 47-year-old manager, Andrew Mackinnon, that he wanted "a free life." Mackinnon looked out the window longingly and replied,

"I only wish I had your years. Then, by God, my lad, I'd go along with ye."

Saying Goodbye

On April 5, 1896, Robert arrived at Queen's Dock in Glasgow to board the ss *Concordia* for the Atlantic crossing—along with 1531 sheep, 339 cattle, and 16 horses. He was one of 12,384 British immigrants who would sail to Canada in 1896.

The ss *Concordia* had been built for Glasgow's Donaldson Brothers in 1881 as a 2544-ton cargo ship with limited passenger accommodations. The three-masted ship was 320 feet long with a 41-foot beam, and it sailed at a speed of 10 knots. It would take about two weeks to sail from Scotland to Montreal, but crossing the Atlantic was still unpredictable and dangerous. (A few months after Robert arrived safely in Canada, the ss *Concordia* hit an iceberg while crossing the Atlantic. And sixteen years later, it was an iceberg collision in the North Atlantic that would sink the *Titanic*.)

Robert's family members were aware of these risks when they went to the dock to see him off. Not knowing when or if they would ever see him again, they remained stoic as they said goodbye. His sixty-year-old father handed him a small package that contained a bible and an ivory handled razor (which Robert used for years until it was stolen in California). As the ship edged away, Robert Sr. stared wistfully at his departing son—it was indeed the last time they would see each other.

Robert recalls the parting in *Ploughman of the Moon*: "Maybe I was doing what he would have loved to have done; for besides being a dreamer I think he would have enjoyed adventure. But his

14

destiny was to bring up ten children on two hundred pounds a year. I cannot reproach him for his failings, for they were my own—laziness, daydreaming, a hatred of authority, and a quick temper. I, too, was of a race of men who don't fit in." Prior to his departure, Robert had visited his three aging aunts to say goodbye, shaking their hands in parting. Still, his aunt Jeannie came to the dock to see him just one more time—she had tears in her eyes, sensing they would never meet again. But Robert's mind was on the adventure ahead of him, not on the goodbyes. Years later, he wrote, "With the selfishness of youth I forgot her care and tenderness."

He promised to write his aunts often, but rarely did. They lived out their lives frugally, in a tiny cottage, scrimping to get by. Robert later regretted not sending them money to make their lives more comfortable. He admitted he hadn't even thought of it, and for that, he was "everlastingly sorry."

The Adventure Begins

Finally, Robert's great adventure was underway. He carried along Robert Louis Stevenson's *An Amateur Emigrant*, and measured his journey against Stevenson's. They had both rebelled against middle-class convention when growing up—Stevenson in Edinburgh, and Robert in Glasgow. Both had also left Scotland to search for adventure in North America. Stevenson had written, "Travel is of two kinds and this voyage of mine across the ocean confirmed both... I was not only travelling out of my country in latitude and longitude, but out of myself."

The Atlantic crossing was uneventful but pleasant. At first, Robert sought the company of the other passengers, listening intently to their stories about Canada. He talked with miners returning to underground coal mines, farm hands, and a hatter who was joining his son on a prairie homestead. But as the voyage progressed, Robert began to avoid the company of others. This was mostly due to the fact that he had no change of clothing or personal care items, and therefore didn't look—or smell—very good. All his clothing and toiletries were stowed away in the ship's luggage section because he had labelled his suitcase incorrectly. "Every day, my collar grew grimier and my chin shaggier. Shabby, unshorn, I shrank into my shell."

After crossing the Atlantic, the ss *Concordia* passed the rocky shores of the Dominion of Newfoundland (it wouldn't be part of Canada for another fifty-three years) before sailing along Quebec's shoreline, which was dotted with quaint houses and villages. Robert would later write that his arrival in Canada was one of the great moments of his life. He was euphoric that he had broken away from his life in Scotland and was venturing into the unknown. "Here I am, a traveller—I who was destined to be a stay-at-home. By my own will I have achieved this."

He landed in Montreal in the early morning hours of April 29 with just five dollars in his pocket, and after buying a few things, had only $1.95 left. But Robert wasn't concerned. He was too focused on the adventures to come. "From now on, every day will be of changing scenes and teeming with new characters. No more rubber-stamp living," he wrote.

The train that was to take the ship's passengers across Canada was already waiting for them near the landing wharf. Robert slept close to the train's toilet so that he would be the first in line in the morning. At daybreak, he changed into his Wild West travelling outfit—an outlandish cowboy get-up that his father had bought for him at an auction. It included chaps, Napoleonic high-heeled boots, and a Mexican sombrero. Indeed, Robert was a striking-looking character as he entertained the other passengers with quick draws of his air gun.

Robert's ticket took him across Canada, right to Vancouver Island. Along the way, he started selling his personal belongings to make some money. First went the Gladstone suitcase for ten dollars. Then, the Harris Tweed suit for six dollars, the air gun for ten dollars, and the camera for fifteen dollars. But he felt it was all worth it; he was young, he was free, and he was on an adventure. From the train window, he surveyed Canada's landscape. He found Ontario fascinating, the prairies delightful, and the small villages with quirky names intriguing. He also marvelled at the rugged peaks, steep canyons, and rushing rivers of the Canadian Rockies.

Robert reached Vancouver in June of 1896, took a ferry to Victoria, and travelled up the island's east coast to the Cowichan Valley. Except for an 18-month absence, Vancouver Island would be Robert's home for the next nine years. It would also be where Robert would later launch his writing career.

CHAPTER

2

Adventure in the Americas

THE COWICHAN VALLEY was already home to a large British
expatriate community when Robert arrived in 1896. There was a
colonial Victorian atmosphere to the area. Afternoon teas, tennis,
dances, and going to church were all big social activities. One of
the oldest tennis clubs in the British Commonwealth—second only
to Wimbledon in England—was founded there in 1887. Called the
South Cowichan Lawn Tennis Club, its members wore white flannel trousers or long white dresses, and took tea on the lawn after a
match. Robert soon became a member.

Underneath the surface of colonial congeniality, Robert sensed
a tension between Cowichan's young male immigrants and its
older male residents. The young men were often "remittance men,"
living on money sent from home. Their lives revolved around

horses, dogs, guns, and fishing—not hard work. The older genera-
tion of men, most of whom were conservative military veterans,
were called "mossbacks," likened to a stone or old tree that was
covered in moss. They were the pioneers who had worked hard to
build the island's communities, and considered themselves British
Columbians. The hard-working mossbacks looked at the remittance men with contempt, while the remittance men thought the
mossbacks were boring and old-fashioned.

Robert's first job in the Cowichan Valley appears to be working for the Colvins, a Scottish family from the Inner Hebrides
(he called them the MacTartans in his memoirs). History would
record that the family matriarch, Jeremenia Colvin, taught Fair
Isle knitting patterns to the Cowichan's Coast Salish women. The
women then developed the knitting style into their world-famous
Cowichan sweaters, examples of which were on display at the 1893
Chicago World's Fair.

Though he and the Colvins' son Magnus became close friends,
Robert didn't stay with the family for long. Instead, he began
working at the Mutter ranch in Somenos (in the Cowichan Valley), which was owned by Major James Mutter, a former magistrate
from Islay, Scotland, and junior partner in a distillery and ware-
houses in Glasgow. Major Mutter and his wife Isabella had arrived
in British Columbia with their six children in 1891.

Robert's romantic notions of ranch work didn't match the reality of toiling on a real ranch like the Mutters. His first task was
to pick stones in order to clear an acre of field; he had to put the
stones in a sack and carry them to the side of the clearing.

Next, he weeded a field of turnips. As he crawled between the
rows, tearing out weeds and young turnip sprouts in the hot sun,

he did some philosophizing. Robert theorized that perhaps the weeds had a right to exist, reasoning they were unwanted only because they were called weeds. Then he considered how society's unwanted people might be viewed as weeds, and that they too might be eliminated. "Poor weeds! Maybe I was one myself."

His thoughts then turned to the young turnips that he yanked out of the ground, sacrificed, so that larger turnips could survive. This made him think of the underdogs of the world. Later, his verses would capture the experiences of the ordinary person, championing the underdogs while celebrating their stories.

Turnip weeding was hard work. Robert's hands became raw and his back ached. He deemed the hardship all worthwhile, however, when he looked up and around at the blue sky, the mountains, and the forests. "Here was a dream world worthy of a dreamer... I hated the grovelling toil. I despised myself for doing it, but—well if it was the price I had to pay for all this beauty, then I was glad to pay it," he later wrote.

Farm labour did have its diversity. Robert hayed, threshed, cleaned manure from a pigsty, and tried unsuccessfully to milk cows. And, all the while, he battled insects—hordes of black flies, sand flies, and mosquitoes. (He even sent a dead mosquito in a letter back to Scotland to show his family.)

He also got the chance to ride a horse, but the scenario turned out a bit differently than he expected. James Jr. "Jock," one of the Mutter sons, encouraged Robert to try riding bareback on a bronco. When Jock hit the bronco's rump, the horse galloped wildly off. For the next mile, Robert tried desperately to hang on while sliding along the horse, finally managing to lock his arms around its neck.

Some time later, he rode horseback to his first afternoon tea at the Mutters. Wanting to look his best, he wore white flannel trousers and his high boots. He fit the romantic image of the rugged cowboy—until he couldn't get off his horse. He was stuck in the saddle. His comical dilemma became the subject of a poem by Jean, the eldest of the Mutter children.

After six months with the Mutters, Robert's work was finished. So, when he heard that a Welsh mossback named Harry "Hank" Evans was looking for a winter companion, he took the job. Robert moved up the island's east coast to Hank's isolated cattle ranch. It was a five-kilometre walk through the bush to reach the ranch, and the nearest neighbour was a half-day hike away.

Hank's frame shack was surrounded by towering Douglas firs, knee-high grass, and old scaffolding. Thirty years earlier, a woman had answered Hank's ad for a bride, and he was going to build a second storey to his home when she arrived. However, she changed her mind at the last minute and never came. Hank never bothered to take down the scaffolding.

During his winter with Hank, Robert slept in a bedroom that had no furniture. Hank, meanwhile, slept in a cubbyhole under the roof. Each night, Robert lay on a buffalo robe and wrapped himself in his thick woollen mackinaw blanket. Each morning, he began his meagre chores. His ranch duties were limited to lighting the morning fire, sweeping the living room, baking bread, and helping Hank feed twenty cattle. In short, he lived a lazy life at Hank's, but it was an "energetically cultivated laziness."

Robert soon gained a reputation as a freeloader. He changed his style of clothing to a black shirt with white tie and black stetson, and softened his Scottish accent. He played Hank's old banjo and became the area's entertainment at parties and social gatherings. Sometimes, just to be a part of a community singsong in a settler's log cabin, he would travel kilometres down a bush trail in the dark. Robert also became an avid reader of Hank's stack of old magazines, studying every page in detail, particularly the articles on California. He developed a strong desire to write, and would sit alone by the fire at night and dream of being a writer.

It was the need for cash that, in the spring, brought Robert back to the outskirts of Duncan to work on a dairy farm owned by George Treffry Corfield. Originally from Cornwall, England, Corfield now owned a 160-hectare ranch, the largest in the valley.

Robert's job was to look after the cows, sometimes for up to sixteen hours a day. He lived in the bunkhouse, along with about a dozen other cowhands. Four nights after moving in, Robert discovered his bunk bed was heavily infested with bedbugs. Upon making this discovery, he dumped the mattress in the river and spent the night in the hay barn. The next day, he got some lumber and built himself a new bed.

By the end of 1897, Robert was restless, ready for another adventure. He had been thinking about California for some time, especially San Francisco, the city where Bret Harte had written his gold rush stories, and where Robert Louis Stevenson had lived briefly. In November, he gave his notice to Corfield (who invited him to come back anytime), and headed for California.

Drifting Through America

A month later, Robert was in Seattle with forty dollars to his name. When he saw a poster advertising a one-dollar, one-way ticket to San Francisco on the ss *Mariposa*, he felt destiny was calling and eagerly paid his fare. His travelling companions were a hundred American hobos, and he listened intently to their colourful stories, storing the material for the day he would write ballads.

The voyage itself was terrible; not only was Robert seasick for much of it, he also had to share a bunk with a Swede and sleep on a bed that was crawling with cockroaches.

On the last night of the voyage, he gathered up his belongings and spent the night on the ship's deck. It was a warm night, with a gentle wind and calm sea. He was looking forward to reaching San Francisco the next day.

Soon after his arrival, Robert sought out Portsmouth Square, in the heart of Chinatown. There, he would sit on a bench and stare at the Stevenson Memorial, feeling inspired by his mentor's spirit. Robert Louis Stevenson had spent many hours sitting in the same square—perhaps even on the same bench that Robert was sitting on. When Stevenson died, a granite pillar topped with a bronze galleon was erected in the square, inscribed with the words from Stevenson's *Christmas Sermon*:

> *To Be Honest, To be Kind—To Earn*
> *a Little, To Spend a Little Less*

San Francisco fueled Robert's imagination. He revelled in its romance, its lustiness, and its vitality. It was filled with Wild West characters who carried guns and weren't afraid to use them. The "ribald brutality" excited him.

He was also intrigued by exotic Chinatown and would spend hours walking its streets and alleys. With its opium dens, joss houses, and brothels, it was unlike anything he had ever seen before. At the waterfront, he had beer with the fishermen and almost signed up for a ship heading for Tahiti. On Kearny and Market streets, he drank in shady bars where the girl "box-workers" plied customers with drinks and then robbed them. On Powell Street, he was conned by a palm reader and got into a fight with a strong-arm enforcer (Robert successfully used the knuckle-duster he had bought for self-protection).

And when Robert needed some quiet time, he would wander back to the Stevenson Memorial, where he would sit and dream about becoming a writer. It was his favourite place in the city.

Robert was enjoying his carefree life, marvelling that he was actually in San Francisco. He had no job, no occupation, and no plan for the future—but that didn't concern him. "I was terribly happy and, though alone, I had no fear of the future. I might be down in the gutter, but I had faith in my star."

But one day, he realized he had only ten dollars left, and it snapped him back into reality. He had been in San Francisco for a month, and now, for the first time, he felt concerned about his financial situation. He was at risk of becoming one of the city's destitute, and it scared him. Though he scoured the want ads to get a job, nothing seemed to appeal to him. He went to an employment agency and was offered a steady job as a handyman for two elderly ladies. His mind said yes to this secure job that could change his life, but he shocked himself when his voice said "No." He just couldn't make a long-term commitment; his urge to wander was too strong.

So instead, he accepted a short-term labourer's position from a contractor in Los Angeles. The job paid two dollars a day, less seventy-five cents for board. The day before Robert was to start, the contractor told him to be at the train station the following morning. Robert didn't know where he was going or what kind of work he would be doing, but he didn't mind—he liked the mystery of the unknown.

The next morning, he boarded a train with several other workers. It was night when the train arrived at Azuza, a small town about forty kilometres from Los Angeles. The workers were taken to a small hotel and, to Robert's surprise, were jeered at along the way as "strikebreakers." In the morning, as they climbed into two stagecoaches, a driver told them they were headed to work in the San Gabriel Canyon. Three hours later, the group was housed in roofless bunkhouses at the workers camp. Robert loved the wildness and the open air—this was his kind of adventure.

The work site itself was located on a small mountain shelf about 270 metres above the camp. Each morning, Robert and three other workers were hauled, by bucket, up to the site to dig a tunnel through the mountain. The low, dark tunnel was lit by candles that were pushed into the dirt walls. Robert's job was to aid another man in lifting four 160-pound boxes of mixed concrete onto a wooden truck bed, push it along makeshift rails through the tunnel to the cement gang, then dump the load and go back for another.

He spent the next ten days working long, brutal hours in the tunnel. Then one night, as he was heading to the bucket to return to camp, he was told the cable had just broken and that some men had been badly injured, possibly even killed. Robert realized it could have been him in the fatal bucket. The next day, he transferred to the gravel gang, and six days later, on Christmas Eve, he quit and headed to Los Angeles with ten dollars in his pocket.

Robert in his wandering years. He commented
later that his pockets were stuffed with books and
papers, and he was a "tough looking case."
QUEEN'S UNIVERSITY ARCHIVES

He lived in a small windowless room at an evangelical mission, and spent much of his time at the public library. To Robert, San Francisco had been a "man's city," inspiring him to write stories in the tradition of Stevenson and Harte, but Los Angeles was like a "gracious woman," inspiring him to write verse. He spent day after day at the library, reading books on poetry. "I wanted to write newspaper poetry, the kind that simple folks clip out and paste in scrap-books," he later explained. He sent some of his poems, including *The Hobo's Lullaby*, to Los Angeles newspapers, and they were quickly printed. These would be Robert's first published works in North America.

Robert drifted from job to job, enduring stints as a saloon dishwasher, a sandwich board man, and an orange picker. He was getting a bit worried about his "shiftless existence" and put an ad in the paper for a job. It read: "Stone-broke in a strange city. Young man. University non-graduate, desires employment of any kind. Understands Latin and Greek. Speaks French, German and Chinook. Knowledge of book-keeping and shorthand; also of Art and Literature. Accept any job, but secretarial work preferred."

Only one offer came in: a job in a brothel for thirty dollars a month. The job included handyman chores, but because of Robert's background, was more focused on bringing some culture to the three ladies of the house. The position was temporary, until the brothel's regular handyman got out of jail. When Robert later left the brothel, one of the ladies gave him a parting gift: her guitar, in a brown leather case.

With the guitar on his back, Robert headed south to Mexico, ending up at Ensenada. After spending ten days there, he walked back to the United States, covering forty-eight kilometres a day. To save on shoe leather, he went barefoot on the highway.

Upon reaching Los Angeles, he felt he had come to another crossroads. "Once more I mused: What is directing my steps? ... Well, a force stronger than myself seemed to be drawing me on to another destiny, and, even though it looked a gloomy one, I must fulfil it." Robert bedded down in a clean, windowless cubicle at the Salvation Army for ten cents a night, and ate beans and hash dinners for five cents a meal (it cost five cents more for bread and an orange). He became one of the hobos of Los Angeles, learning from them how to survive. Soon, however, he grew disenchanted with their lifestyle and tried to think of ways he could get out of the gutter. He was too proud to write home to ask for money. Instead, he trusted fate with his destiny, musing, "What will be must be."

He took on work as a labourer, digging to make a tramway tunnel. On his first day, two men died on the job, prompting Robert to quit at the end of his shift. Still, the poignant experience inspired him to write his famous ballad, *The Song of the Wage-Slave*.

Next, Robert tried being a hotel dishwasher, but was quickly fired. He was beginning to feel like a failure in life when, sitting on a park bench, he happened to read a newspaper headline heralding the news of the Klondike Gold Rush: "A Ton of Gold Comes out of Frozen North." Suddenly, he knew he would be the Klondike poet, writing evocative, descriptive verse about the quest for gold, just like Bret Harte had done in 1849 with the California Gold Rush. But the time was not yet—he had some travelling to do first.

Robert wandered through the American southwest states of Utah, Texas, Arizona, Nevada, and Colorado. He took on odd jobs, like weeding a lemon grove (five dollars for the week) or other casual labour. Sometimes he played his guitar and sang cowboy songs in exchange for a meal and lodgings. Seldom did he exceed his planned budget of five dollars a month.

He was a "wandering minstrel," and with a packet of tea in his packsack, he was truly enjoying the drifter lifestyle. And then a train almost killed him. He was crossing a train bridge with trestles in Southern California when he heard the train coming. Fighting his rising panic, he realized there was only one way to save himself: he would have to quickly drop his packsack and guitar and crawl onto a jutting beam. The move saved his life, but his guitar was smashed on the rocks below.

Shaken, Robert returned to Los Angeles. When he saw his old hobo friends again, he suddenly feared the thought of becoming like them. The life of the hobo had truly lost its lustre. He decided to return to Vancouver Island, and left on a northbound boat soon after. He had been in the United States for about eighteen months, and later wrote, "Much of my wayfaring was monotonous and is now vague in my memory... I had moments, too, when, wet and weary, I would feel very wretched. Then I would say: If only my mother could look on me now, it's sorry she'd feel for her boy."

Three weeks later, sometime in the middle of 1898, he was back working at the Corfield ranch in the Cowichan Valley. He would stay there for the next four years, during which time he wrote his first serious verse.

3

Back in Canada

AT FIRST, ROBERT was given the job of swineherd at the Corfield ranch, and he didn't mind it. "Pigs are often preferable to people. I can see poetry in a pigsty…" In the autumn, he was promoted to cattleman, looking after fifty cows and twenty calves. Initially, he liked his new position, but by December he was convinced he was meant for greater things. He wanted to get back to a white-collar job.

Destiny did come knocking, but in a violent way. In December of 1898, a terrible accident almost killed him. Robert was leading a big black Holstein bull to pasture when suddenly the animal charged him and savagely knocked him to the ground. Another ranch hand saw the accident and quickly leapt the fence to distract the rampaging bull, giving Robert a chance to crawl to safety.

Robert spent four years of his life working for the Corfield family
in Cowichan, first as a cowhand on their ranch and then as a
storekeeper in their general store and post office, pictured above.
COWICHAN VALLEY MUSEUM AND ARCHIVES

With two broken ribs, it looked unlikely that Robert could continue cattle hustling with the Corfields. But luckily for him, the
storekeeper job at the Corfield's General Store and Post Office had
just become vacant. Robert applied and became the new storekeeper. He was elated. "I have had great moments in my life—when
it seemed the gates of Heaven opened wide and I stepped through
them from the depths of hell. This was one of them."

For the next four years, Robert had a set, but active, routine. He
opened the store every morning at nine o'clock. Half an hour later,
he hitched the pony to the wagon to collect cans of cream from
the farmers and deliver mailbags to the train station. After going

to the creamery to unload the cans and reload with empty ones, he stopped again at the station to pick up the incoming mail. Back in the store by noon, he sorted and distributed the mail, and then went for lunch. He spent the afternoon in the store, hating that he had to sell inferior goods to the Indigenous customers. He called the trading and selling "petty huckstering" and later wrote, "Occasional customers would come in, but I would serve them without enthusiasm." His duties outside the store included maintaining the tennis courts, tutoring the Corfields' seven sons, and butchering sheep and cattle.

It was not the rugged cowboy life he had originally envisioned, but it required very little hard work—and he liked that. Robert now had time to enjoy a social life in Cowichan. He sang in the church choir, went to parties, read novels, and became active in amateur theatre. He also rode horses, swam in the Koksilak River, went salmon fishing, and learned to shoot. And, most importantly, he began to write some of his best poetry.

Robert's famous literary career actually began while he was a storekeeper in British Columbia. It started with a chance meeting in 1899, when a newspaper editor by the name of Charles Harrison Gibbons dropped into the Corfield store one day. While chatting, he learned that Robert wrote verse and asked if he could read some of his work. "One item was a four-page pulsating human interest bit—minor Boer war incident, worked up artistically, that gripped," Gibbons later recalled. "I said to him, 'Give me this Bob for the Sunday paper'."

Robert objected at first, saying, "Oh, it isn't worth printing in a newspaper." But Gibbons insisted, and a ballad entitled *The Christmas Card* appeared in the Victoria's *Daily Colonist* on December 27,

1899—the first publication of his work in Canada. At the time, there was great public interest in the Second Boer War being fought in South Africa. *The Christmas Card* was a sentimental ballad about a child's Christmas card to his soldier father fighting in South Africa, but the card arrives after the father dies in battle.

By June, Robert had written a total of six war ballads, each dealing with the horror of the Boer War and its human cost and sacrifice. The last of the six ballads, *The March of the Dead*, is haunting and timeless, its message still relevant today. Written in the collective voice of the dead soldiers, it asks the reader not to forget them as they return home, marching invisibly as a ghost battalion alongside the surviving veterans.

There was a personal, emotional connection for Robert with the Boer War. His brother Alexander ("Alick") was captured by the Boers on November 15, 1899, along with Winston Churchill. Churchill escaped, but Alick was held prisoner for two years in Pretoria.

Robert's war ballads were popular, and eagerly published by the *Daily Colonist* and other newspapers. After public interest in the Boer War subsided, Robert continued to write verse, this time about life on Vancouver Island and around Cowichan. These ballads included *Music in the Bush*, *The Little Old Log Cabin*, and *Song of the Social Failure*.

Poet in Love

In late November of 1902, the 28-year-old Robert fell in love with a young schoolteacher named Constance "Connie" M. MacLean, the daughter of the first mayor of Vancouver, Malcolm A. MacLean. They met when she was visiting her cousin, Dr. Dallas Perry, who

The Imperial Bank of Commerce at Fort and Government
Streets in Victoria, where Robert worked briefly.
HERITAGE HOUSE COLLECTION

practised in the Cowichan Valley. It was love at first sight. Two
days after their first meeting, Robert wrote a poem for her called
The Coming of Miss McLean. And when they danced the following
weekend, it was the beginning of a strong relationship that would
last until 1908.

Robert now had a new focus. He started thinking seriously
about what he should be doing with his life. He had little to offer
the woman he loved. Besides, after four years at the Corfield ranch,
he was getting restless and feeling stagnant. "I saw clearly that my

easy life was not getting me anywhere. I felt a slacker, a bit of a waster. I was approaching middle age, and I realized with a shock that my position in the world was negligible. I was a square peg in a succession of round holes," he later wrote.

He decided to save his money to go to university, perhaps become a teacher. In the spring of 1903, he resigned as Corfield's store-keeper and took a temporary job doing road construction. At night, he studied by candlelight for the university matriculation exams.

But his mind strayed back to writing verse, and he composed one of his most tender poems, *Apart and Yet Together*, inspired by his relationship with Connie. It was published in December 1903 in *Munsey's Magazine*, and Robert received five dollars for the pub-lication, a healthy compensation for a half-hour's work.

Soon after, he passed the university matriculation exams and began his studies at the University of Victoria. But, just as he had in Glasgow, Robert realized he was not suited to the discipline of academia, or to accepting the authority of the professors. Once again, he abandoned his studies.

Money was tight. He only had enough to last about two weeks in Victoria. He wondered when his guardian angel would save him, and as always, his angel took care of his needs. On October 10, 1903, Robert started a job as a bank clerk with the Canadian Impe-rial Bank of Commerce at the corner of Fort and Government Streets in Victoria. Since he was the most junior of the clerks, he was assigned to live in a furnished apartment above the bank's vault room. A trapdoor in his bedroom floor opened onto the two-tiered bank vault. He was expected to sleep with a gun by his side, serving as the bank's security guard after hours.

Back in Canada

With his first paycheque, Robert bought a piano and a dinner jacket, as bank clerks received numerous invitations to parties and dances. Less than six months later, he was given permanent status and a raise of ten pounds, and was then transferred to Kamloops, a small town of 2,000 people in the interior of British Columbia. He settled in to his new home, bought a banjo and a pony, and took up polo. He also wrote many letters to Connie, who was living in Vancouver.

A year later, the bank transferred Robert to Whitehorse. It was a cold November day in 1904 when he sailed out on the Canadian Pacific Steamer *Prince Beattie*, headed for Skagway, Alaska. From Skagway, he would take a train to Whitehorse. "I had an idea that a new and wonderful chapter in my life was about to begin," he wrote in *Ploughman of the Moon*.

Whitehorse Years

As the *Prince Beattie* steamed through the Inside Passage towards Skagway, Robert mused about how great life would be if one didn't have to work, if one could live at the expense of others. During the five-day voyage, he reflected on an economic plan to accomplish such a scenario. The key was getting enough capital to generate a monthly interest income. He calculated that savings of $5,000 at five percent annual interest would give him a monthly income of $20 — sufficient for his needs, and perhaps supplemented by some writing.

This would become the core of what he called his "Escape Idea." Saving $5,000 could bring him freedom from working.

Whitehorse is located at the southern tip of Lake Laberge. The northern end of the lake empties into a tributary of the Yukon

River, which then flows 3200 kilometres to the Bering Sea. During the Klondike Gold Rush, when Whitehorse was booming, over 7,000 boats—from sternwheelers to kayaks—traversed Lake Laberge.

When Robert arrived in 1904, the boom was long over. Whitehorse was a struggling town with less than 1,000 people. Log cabins, false-fronted stores, and government offices filled the main street. Nearby was a graveyard of broken-down lake steamers, all abandoned after the gold rush. The excitement of the boom years was still fresh in the memories of Whitehorse residents, but the city had a ghost-town look.

When the coatless Robert stepped onto the wooden platform at the train station in Whitehorse, his new boss, Leonard De Gex, was there greet him. Dressed in a fur coat, the bank manager took one look at Robert and ordered him to bundle up.

Robert replied, "I'm not cold. How cold is it?"

"About thirty below. You don't feel it because you are a cheechako. Your blood's like soup. When you've been here a year you'll get cold-conscious." (Cheechako means "greenhorn" in Chinook)

De Gex then took Robert to his home. Robert and another teller, Harold Tylor, would be boarding with the bank manager and his wife. In his memoirs, Robert wrote that those early years in Whitehorse were the happiest periods of his life, commenting, "For I found a real home such as I had not enjoyed since I left my own." The young and pretty Mrs. De Gex looked after her "boys" like a seasoned mother, prompting Robert to later write, "Few real families of four were more united and happy."

But while Robert was happy, others in the community were facing tough times. Like many frontier towns, Whitehorse was built mainly of wood, so fire was a constant danger to its existence. In the early morning hours of May 23, 1905, everyone in town was called into action when flames threatened the entire downtown section.

The blaze started in Eddie Marcotte's barbershop, in the back of the old Windsor Hotel. The volunteer fire department had received its new boiler pump the day before, but no one had been adequately trained in its use. The fire engine broke down after a few minutes of operation, and within two hours of the start of the fire, most of Whitehorse's business district was destroyed.

Robert remembers the blaze in *Ploughman of the Moon*: "Men were yelling frantically for water... I heard a shout of panic: 'There's no more water in the tanks. He's let them run dry. We're lost, we can't fight the fire!' Despair fell on the milling crowd... And there they stood staring at those limp hose pipes from which no water came. We were helpless and, even as we looked, the fire, as if in triumph, shot out a great blaze of flame that dominated the smoke."

Then De Gex yelled to Robert, "Come on. The bank's in danger." The bank staff, including Robert, ran to the bank building. They watered down the bank's walls in an effort to prevent sparks and the intense heat of the blaze from igniting. As the employees lugged buckets of water from four huge barrels of rainwater, the building across the street suddenly burst into flames. Frantically, everyone kept watering the bank's walls, ultimately saving their building. In the end, Robert's bank was one of the few buildings to survive. But, ever resourceful, the people of Whitehorse had their town rebuilt within four months.

Within a year, Robert was promoted to bank teller, had saved $1,000, and was active in the Whitehorse social scene. He successfully produced a play called *The Area Belle*, and was known around town for his lively recitations of ballads such as *Casey at the Bat* and *The Face on the Barroom Floor*.

When Robert was asked to recite at a church social, the editor of the *Whitehorse Star*, Elmer "Stroller" White, suggested he present one of his own compositions. Robert thought about it as he went for one of his long woodland walks. He liked the idea of writing a dramatic ballad for recitation, but struggled to come up with a theme. Then, one Saturday night while he walking by the busy and noisy bar scene, the ballad's opening lines suddenly appeared in his mind: "A bunch of the boys were whooping it up."

He quickly walked back to the bank building, crept downstairs to his teller's cage, and started work on his ballad. But disaster was looming: the ledger-keeper in the guardroom thought Robert was a burglar, and he shot at him. As Robert later wrote in his autobiography, "Fortunately [the ledger-keeper] was a poor shot or the *Shooting of Dan McGrew* might never have been written... Anyhow, with the sensation of a bullet whizzing past my head, and a detonation ringing in my ears, the ballad was achieved."

Robert wrote the ballad as if a spirit was dictating the words to him—it flowed effortlessly, stanza after stanza. Exhausted, he finished at 5 AM and went to bed. He had written the ballad to recite at the church concert, but in the end, couldn't use it "owing to the cuss-words." So he put it away in a drawer.

The steamer *Olive May* is believed to have been
the boat on which the cremation that inspired one of Robert
Service's most famous poems took place.
HERITAGE HOUSE COLLECTION

A month later, Robert heard a strange tale about a man being
cremated in an abandoned boat. According to those who knew
Robert at the time, the story was told to him by the town's doctor,
Leonard "Doc" Sugden. The doctor had gone to attend to an "old
Swede" who was seriously ill on the shores of Lake Laberge, about
fifty kilometres north of Whitehorse.

The Swede was already dead when Sugden had reached him,
and, being alone, the doctor couldn't bring the man's body all
the way back to Whitehorse. Nearby on the shore was an old
derelict steamer called the *Olive May*. Sugden claimed he had

Dr. Leonard "Doc" Sugden performed the cremation that
inspired one of Robert Service's most famous poems..
PHOTO COURTESY OF DOROTHY SUGDEN

disposed of the body by putting it in the boiler of the old boat and cremating it.

Robert had listened intently to the man who'd cremated the Swede, and later wrote of the moment, "I had a feeling that here was a decisive moment of destiny." Indeed, the doctor's story would soon become immortalized in one of Robert's greatest ballads, *The Cremation of Sam McGee*.

Writing this ballad came easily to Robert. "I took the woodland trail, my mind seething with excitement and a strange ecstasy," he said in his autobiography. "As I started in: *There are strange things done in the midnight sun* ... verse after verse developed with scarce a check ... For six hours I tramped those silver glades and when I rolled happily into bed, my ballad was cinched. Next day, with scarcely any effort of memory I put it on paper. My moonlight improvisation was secure, and though I did not know it, 'McGee' was to be the keystone of my success." The two ballads, *The Shooting of Dan McGrew* and *The Cremation of Sam McGee* would become the most famous—and most recited—ballads in modern history.

Robert's imagination was now swirling, creating new verse every day. His ballads told powerful stories with drama and humour. He was inspired by the people he met, the stories he heard, and the landscapes he walked. After creating his ballads, Robert would file each one and, according to his memoirs, forget about them, saying "[Writing] was just a diversion, maybe a foolish one ... I did it with no thought of publication."

In late 1906, Robert gathered his poems into a manuscript and gave them to Mrs. De Gex to read. She suggested he get them printed as books of verse to give to friends. He called his little book *Songs of a Sourdough*—he liked alliteration and it seemed a fitting title, as he was now officially a sourdough (someone who has seen the Yukon River freeze in the fall and thaw in the spring). He then looked to Toronto for a publisher that would print the books for $100.

By this time, his family was living in Toronto after having immigrated to Canada the previous year. Robert sent the manuscript, plus a cheque for $100, to his father in Toronto to bring to the Methodist Book and Publishing House for printing. The company was the largest book publisher in Canada at the time and was headed by William Briggs.

Robert's manuscript reached Briggs in December, and he was impressed. He arranged for a set of galley proofs of *Songs of a Sourdough* to be given to his salesman, Robert Bond, who was about to leave by train on his annual western sales trip. Briggs apparently told the 23-year-old Bond to try to sell some of Robert's work.

Bond was already packed, but at the last minute shoved the proofs into his pocket. On the train, while sitting in the dining car, he remembered the proofs and read them. He laughed out loud as he read—the poems were so unusual, so Canadian. A neighbouring diner asked Bond to read him the poems. Later, in the smoking car, Bond recited *The Cremation of Sam McGee* to a crowd of passengers. They loved it.

The first stopover on the westward train was in Fort William, Ontario, a small frontier town on the western shore of Lake Superior. Bond decided to see if he could interest the local bookseller, John McKenzie, in ordering copies of *Songs of a Sourdough*.

The salesman walked the short distance from the Canadian Pacific Railway station on Hardisty Street to Flatt & McKenzie, a fancy goods and jewellery store on Simpson Street. McKenzie had given him an hour to show his wares in the sample room. When Bond mentioned a new book of Canadian poetry, McKenzie said, "We'll skip that," but added that he would consider the more saleable poetry collections, like W. H. Drummond's *Habitant* poems.

Bond returned to the store later, and again asked McKenzie about the new poetry book. To his surprise, McKenzie responded, "Is this the poetry you were reading on the train to some travellers? They told me about it." Bond said yes, and started reciting *The Cremation of Sam McGee*, but stopped when customers came in the store. The bookseller then ordered five copies, giving Fort William (now part of the City of Thunder Bay) the honour of becoming the world's first place to buy *Songs of a Sourdough*.

By the time Bond reached British Columbia in early March 1907, he had already sold out the first run of 500 copies. The publisher then sent Robert a long letter, returning his $100 cheque and offering him a royalty contract. When Robert got the letter, he assumed Briggs was sending his cheque back because he did not want to print the book. When he finally read the letter later in the day, he was elated, and quickly telegraphed back his acceptance. Soon after, *Songs of a Sourdough* became the first commercially successful book of Canadian poetry. A reviewer in *Saturday Night* called Robert the "Canadian Kipling."

When Robert received his copies of the book, he was in awe. He wrote that he "caressed the bratleg of my muse ... like the rapture of a mother over her first-born." Indeed, he felt he had achieved immortality with the publication of *Songs of a Sourdough*. Later in the year, the book was published in the United States (under the title *The Spell of the Yukon and Other Verses*), and in Great Britain. *Songs of a Sourdough* was a bestseller worldwide.

Robert sent a copy of the book to Gibbons, the first Canadian editor to publish his work, with a little note: "They've caught on amazingly though only the Lord knows why. They're rough and ready slapstick stuff for the most part and you'll agree dashed off to please the gang. Some day I mean to write something worth while— real high brow stuff that people will talk about with upturned eyes and praise prodigiously, though it will probably have no meaning to them or anyone else."

In Whitehorse, reaction to the book was mixed. Robert remembered, "Many thought me a presumptuous young pup to exploit the town to my profit... No one saw in it a record-breaking success." It was only when the town's summer citizens returned and told everyone how popular the book was in the south that the book's success was recognized by the townspeople. Robert became an instant celebrity and one of Whitehorse's most popular tourist attractions.

In the autumn of 1907, Robert became eligible for a three-month bank leave with pay, and the bank insisted he take the long holiday. He returned to Vancouver, pleased he could spend time again with Connie. All future volumes of *Songs of a Sourdough* were dedicated to Connie, reading, "To C.M."

Despite their time apart, the couple's five-year relationship appeared to be strong. While Robert was in Vancouver, they spent plenty of time together, but then something went wrong. When his bank leave was over, Robert was posted to Dawson City, and the relationship with Connie ended. To this day, no one has spoken about what caused the breakup.

Dawson City

Robert was to report to Dawson City on April 8, 1908. He looked forward to returning to and writing about the North. "I felt I had another book in me and would be desperate if I did not get a chance to do it. I wanted to write the story of the Yukon from the inside, and the essential story of the Yukon was that of the Klondike." His journey to get there would take him by steamer to Skagway, by train to Whitehorse, and finally by sleigh to Dawson City.

It was late March by the time he arrived in Whitehorse. The snow was still deep, and the Yukon River frozen. Temperatures were in the range of –30 degrees. Robert was booked on the White Pass Stage to travel the Overland Trail to Dawson City. Advertised as a first-class relay stage line, it ran almost 650 kilometres along the frozen wilderness between Whitehorse and Dawson City.

Drawn by teams of four to six horses, a one-way journey between Whitehorse and Dawson City took anywhere from three to ten days to complete on the frozen Yukon River and surrounding area. Between 200 and 275 horses were used in the winter along the Overland Trail, with each trip using an average of 15 teams. Travel was only during daylight; at night, passengers boarded at one of the roadhouses along the trail. The roadhouses were crude log buildings, their roofs covered with moss and dirt for insulation.

Robert said he didn't realize the vastness of the land until he spent long days on the open sleigh, with temperatures dipping to −34 degrees Celsius. "Our breath froze on our fur collars; our lashes and eyebrows were hoar; our cheeks pinky bright, as we took shallow breaths of Arctic air. Every now and then the driver would have to break icicles out of the nostrils of the horses." When the sleigh tipped over, Robert and the passengers had to stand in the waist-deep snowdrifts and push.

Each day, three or four scheduled stops were made at outposts spaced about thirty-five kilometres apart. At each stop, passengers ate and rested while the teams of horses were changed. Robert noted, "As we had no exercise, we suffered from surfeited stomachs and had to take laxatives."

Passengers dressed warmly for these journeys: fur coats, fur hats with nose and ear protectors, and well-insulated footwear such as felt shoes and moccasins. White Pass Stage provided buffalo robes and a heated metal box on the floor to keep the feet warm (it burned coal or was stuffed with heated brick). In *Ploughman of the Moon*, Robert wrote, "Day after day... we hunched in our coon coats, half doped by the monotony of bitter brightness." Six days after leaving Whitehorse by sleigh, he arrived in a dark Dawson City.

American Joe Ladue founded Dawson City in 1896, the same year that gold was discovered twenty kilometres away on Bonanza Creek (also the same year that Robert sailed to Canada). For many years, Ladue had been a trader, sawmill operator, and prospector along the Yukon River. He was a man of vision who was always one step ahead of the gold rushes, ready to supply miners with whatever they needed. When he heard about the Bonanza Creek gold find, he loaded lumber from his sawmill on a raft, drifted down the Klondike River, and, on August 28, 1896, staked the boggy flats

Dawson City was bustling with a population of about 40,000 people at the peak of the gold rush in 1898. When Robert Service arrived ten years later, the population had dwindled to only 4,000 people, though gold mining was still a staple industry there.

NAC C-6648

northeast of the mouth. Within days, he registered the townsite of Dawson and by early October, he moved his sawmill to Dawson City, selling building lots and rough lumber at $140 per 1,000 feet to miners working the gold rush at Bonanza Creek. The original settlement in 1896 had twenty-five men and one woman; in 1898, at the peak of the gold rush, Dawson City had a population of 40,000 and was the largest Canadian city west of Winnipeg.

When Robert arrived ten years later, the population had plummeted to 4,000, but gold mining was still the town's main industry.

The staff of the Imperial Bank of Commerce in Dawson on June 22, 1908. Robert Service is standing at the back, in front of the window.
HERITAGE HOUSE COLLECTION

He stayed in the bank's boarding house, along with a dozen other bachelors. At that time, his annual salary of $900 was easily surpassed by his royalties of $4,000 for *Songs of a Sourdough*.

An observer of people, Robert continued gathering stories, finding his membership in the Arctic Brotherhood particularly worthwhile. The Arctic Brotherhood is said to have begun in February 1899 on the luxury steamship *City of Seattle* as it was sailing to Skagway. A group of passengers were discussing the North's "benevolent spirit of helpfulness," and someone suggested this spirit be recognized in the formation of a "great social brotherhood of the North." The idea was enthusiastically received, and the name Arctic Brotherhood was chosen.

The brotherhood developed an initiation ritual, a council, by-laws, and a constitution. Members were expected to help each other and to not "abuse or ill-treat" animals such as dogs and horses (giving recognition to their importance to a miner). To foster cordial relations between Canada and the United States (who were disputing northern boundaries), the society took as its motto "no boundary lines here," and covered all of Alaska, Yukon, the Northwest Territories, and British Columbia north of the 54th parallel. Thousands joined the brotherhood, including the most active and prominent men of the North. Robert enjoyed socializing with them at the Arctic Brotherhood's hall, admitting, "I wormed their stories out of them and tucked away many a colourful yarn."

In the winter, he wrote every night from midnight to 3 AM, determined to complete his second volume of verse within four months. He worked out a writing plan: he would sleep from 9 PM to midnight, get up and make a pot of strong black tea, and set to work.

His second volume of verse, entitled *Ballads of a Cheechako*, was a planned and constructed volume. He had to work at it, rather than rely on inspiration. "Instead of my joyous exuberance, I blasted out my rhyme with grim determination," he recalled later. "It was a product of midnight oil—luckless effort, a second book, written to follow-up the success of the first."

Ballads of a Cheechako, published in 1909, contained twenty-one ballads on eighty-eight pages. It included verse like *To the Man of the High North, Pious Pete, Gum-boot Pete, Muckluck Meg, The Prospector*, and ended with *Envoi*. While his first book of verse included poems he had written in British Columbia and California, his second book was verse he had written about Yukon while he was in Yukon. It was eagerly anticipated by his readers, and was as successful as his first book.

By this time, Robert's "Escape Idea" economic plan was working quite well. He'd accomplished fairly easily his plan to save $5,000, and now decided to start a second plan: he would quit the bank when he had saved $10,000.

For the next two years, he did no further writing, but his royalty cheques kept coming. He continued working at the bank, enjoying his daily two-hour walks after work, and opted for an active social life. He attended skating parties at the outdoor rinks, torchlight snow-shoe parties, sing-along sleigh rides, twice-weekly dances, frequent balls, and fishing expeditions. He recited at concerts and helped with dramatic shows. "It was a glorious time... not much work, lots of fun, money flowing in," he later recalled.

It was while fishing on the nearby Klondike River that he came up with the idea of writing a novel about the gold rush. He reflected that the most colourful episode in the Yukon should be put into fiction form, and figured that no other writer knew the Yukon as he did. He told himself, "There's your chance. It's really up to you." The more Robert thought about it, the more he felt destined to write the novel. His two successful books gave him the confidence. He philosophized, "If one thinks one can do a thing, and tries hard enough, one generally can."

Robert began to make research plans for his Klondike novel: he would talk to the old "sourdoughs" and get their stories. He would get to know their stories so well that they would become real in his mind. He would feel their pain and joy. He felt driven to "recreate a past that would otherwise be lost forever."

When winter came, he was ready to tackle the project—but could do nothing. "My words came with difficulty, my imagination lagged. Something was wrong." He realized the problem was that he needed to be alone, cut off from contact with others. He needed seclusion to immerse himself in writing.

As he mulled over how to accomplish this, an unexpected opportunity was presented to him. He was offered a promotional transfer to Whitehorse, but while it sounded promising, he knew it was the wrong time for him to leave Dawson City. He told his bank manager that effective November 15, 1909, he would no longer be an employee at the bank. When the bank manager asked how much he was earning a year, Robert told him $5,000 from royalties and $1,000 from the bank. The manager agreed with his decision to resign, saying, "Grasp your opportunities. The trouble is we bankers don't get any."

Later, Robert had second thoughts about his decision. He worried about being foolish, too impulsive. But when he received his bank statement, it showed his savings had topped $10,000. He had reached the second economic goal of his "Escape Idea," and could now live on his interest income and be free from working.

Because he could no longer board at the bank's lodgings, Robert had to find a new place to stay. He moved to a rustic hillside cabin that had a pair of moose antlers hanging over the door. The log cabin was sparsely furnished; the sitting room had a small table, two chairs, and a stove, and the bedroom had a double bed. Robert hung photos on the wall, painted the sitting room a pale

Robert Service sitting at his desk in his cabin in Dawson City
YUKON ARCHIVES, GILLIS FAMILY FONDS, 4534

blue, and set to work. His little cabin overlooking the Klondike Valley would be his home for two years.

The winter nights were bitterly cold—so cold that sometimes Robert's blanket, tucked close to his face, would become caked with ice from his breath. One cold night, he went out to the porch to get wood to keep the fire burning in the stove, and accidentally locked himself out. It was –15 degrees Celsius, and he was only wearing his pajamas. The locked front door was too strong to break down, so he went to the back door and successfully rammed it open with his shoulder.

In April 1910, *Trail of the Ninety-Eight* was ready to be sent to Robert's publisher in New York. But Robert became concerned about sending it in the mail, fearing the manuscript would get lost and his work would be gone forever. He decided to deliver it personally, as he had plenty of money to give himself a nice trip.

At first, New York awed him, but by the time he had revised his book to please the publisher, he had grown tired of the city. As a theatrical gesture to show his hardiness as a Yukoner, he told his publisher he was going to walk to New Orleans—and then set about to do it. The weather was terrible—rain, sleet, and snow—and he often got stranded in small towns, where he was forced to stay in dreary rooming houses. Three weeks into the walk, he reached Pennsylvania, and bought a first-class train ticket to New Orleans.

Robert was seeking adventure, something different, but didn't find it in New Orleans. He went on to Havana, Cuba, but became bored and longed for the "snow and tonic air of the North."

By chance, he came across an article in an American magazine titled, "I Had a Good Mother." Then he had an idea: he would go to visit his own mother. "Suddenly I thought: I, too, had a perfectly good mother. She was living in Alberta and I had not seen her in 13 years." His father had died in January 1909, but not before seeing the success of *Songs of a Sourdough*.

Robert decided his next adventure would be to get to know his family again. The family had moved to a homestead in Scotstoun, Alberta, and that's where he headed.

Scotstoun

It was a cold winter day in early February 1911 when Robert surprised his family by knocking on the farmhouse door, pretending to be a salesman. Of course, his charade didn't fool his mother. "Well, if it isn't our Willie," she said.

He spent the next three and a half months on the Service homestead, getting to know his family again. Still at home were his three sisters (Agnes, Jane, and Janet), and three of his six brothers (Stanley, Peter, and Albert). Eventually, Stanley would go to medical school and be a doctor in Toronto, Peter would head to Vancouver to open a second-hand bookshop, and Albert would be killed overseas while fighting in the First World War.

In the spring of 1911, the need for travel and adventure prompted Robert to explore Alberta on foot. He covered 320 kilometres, stopping each night in "Norwegian, Romanian, Slav or French settlements." But this still wasn't enough to satisfy his wanderlust. Canada's North was drawing him like a magnet. He had to go back one more time to finish writing about the area. This time, he wanted to return to Dawson City via the same gold rush route that Klondikers had travelled between 1898 and 1899. He would take the 3,200-kilometre Edmonton Trail to Dawson City, travelling the waterways of the Athabasca, Slave, and Mackenzie Rivers to the Arctic, and then down the Bell, Porcupine, and Yukon Rivers to Dawson City. This all-Canadian water route to the Klondike was half the distance of the American route.

Before now, Robert had created his ballads about the rigours of the North while sitting in a comfortable cabin. Now he would actually live as the Klondikers and wilderness adventurers had. He was thirty-seven years old and in good health, but was the bank-clerk-turned-poet ready to be a real rugged northerner?

CHAPTER

4

The Old Edmonton
Trail to the Klondike

ROBERT STARTED HIS journey by walking 320 kilometres from his family's homestead in Scotstoun to Edmonton, where on May 22, 1911, he boarded a stagecoach to Athabasca Landing, 160 kilometres to the north. It was a two-day trip with an overnight stop at a roadhouse.

The stagecoach passengers included George Mellis Douglas, his brother Lionel, and Dr. August Sandberg from Sweden. The threesome was headed to the Arctic on a mining expedition; they would be searching for minerals in the watershed of the Coppermine River above the Arctic Circle.

These were no ordinary prospectors. George, a lean, muscular, six-foot tall engineer, was a pioneer in northern mineral exploration and development, and one of the first Barren Land explorers to

Robert Service, writing on a piece of paper on his knee, sits in
the stern of an HBC scow travelling down the Athabasca River.
GEORGE DOUGLAS/LAC PA-145196

extensively photograph the Northwest Territories and the region's
Inuit people. His book, *Land Forlorn*, describes their 1911–1912 trip,
and is considered one of the classics of northern literature. George's
brother Lionel (who went to sea at the age of sixteen) was working at the time for the Canadian Pacific Railway (CP), sailing the
trans-Pacific route between Vancouver and Asia. Later, he became
commander of the trans-Pacific RMS *Empress of Asia*, *Canada*, and
Japan steamships, and eventually the general superintendent of CP
Steamships. Dr. Sandberg was a chemist, metallurgist, and geolo-
gist, and although not a trained canoeist, he had good trail and
survival skills, honed by his travels through remote parts of Mexico.

As they were all headed up north together, a friendship developed between the Douglas brothers and Robert. At Athabasca Landing, they intended to get passage on the Hudson's Bay Company scows, known as the "Athabasca Brigade," going to Fort McMurray, but they arrived too late and the brigade had already left. The Douglas group decided to paddle their canoes to catch and board the scow brigade. They invited Robert, a novice canoeist, to join them. For the rest of his life, George delighted in telling how he taught Robert to canoe.

The Athabasca

Athabasca Landing, located at the southernmost point of the Athabasca River, was the transportation hub for freight, pioneers, and explorers entering Canada's Northwest. The landing was the "gateway to the north," and the Athabasca River, Canada's seventh longest, was its highway.

Eleven years earlier at Athabasca Landing, a steady stream of Klondikers were passing through on their way to the Yukon gold fields. A tent city stretching for three kilometres was erected along both riverbanks. One side was named East Chicago and the other West Chicago—Chicago gold seekers outnumbered the others four to one. And, just down from the Hudson's Bay Company post, there was a line of shacks called Bohemian Row.

When Robert and the Douglas group arrived in 1911, Athabasca Landing was still a boomtown with a "huddle of shacks." They found the hotels were all booked, so Robert and his travelling companions stayed overnight on the floor in the backroom of a Chinese "hash joint." Dinner was at the hotel's noisy

The scows of the Athabasca brigade, pulled up to shore for a break.
GEORGE DOUGLAS / LAC PA-145199

dining room, where Robert got the last seat, next to a "grizzly old-timer."

Wherever Robert travelled, he had the uncanny knack of meeting or hearing about an area's most colourful or legendary people. At Athabasca Landing, he heard the stories about Louis (Loison) Fosseneuve, also known as the "King of the Scowmen" or "Captain Shot." It was said that everyone from "Edmonton to the North Pole" knew Louis by sight or reputation, and that just the mention of his name "... could hush a noisy crowd or stop a barroom brawl." He looked like a gunslinger from the American Wild West, six foot three, with hawk-like features, a scraggy beard, and piercing eyes. He left his mark on Alberta history when, in 1867, he was the first man to run a scow through the treacherous Grand Rapids while transporting five Grey Nuns. He is most likely the model for Robert's legendary poem, *Athabasca Dick*.

During his stay at Athabasca Landing, Robert also met the famous Jim Cornwall, better known as "Peace River Jim." He later described this meeting in his autobiography: "I was introduced ... and right there I met the great man of the Mackenzie. Just as Joe Boyle was King of the Yukon, so Jim Cornwall was Lord of the Athabasca. They were similar type, stalwart and handsome. With their strong frames and bold features, they might have been Roman emperors. They typified all that the word Man implies. Both were pioneers, fearless, confident, dominating. And here I wish to pay tribute to two of the great men of the High North— Klondike Joe and Peace River Jim."

Born in Brantford, Ontario, in 1869, Jim had arrived in Alberta in 1896. He was part of the Yukon gold rush, but returned to Peace

River country and settled in the area. A river pilot, he opened fur-trading posts and later formed the Northern Transportation Company, running steamships on the Athabasca and Slave Rivers. When Robert first met him, Jim was the area's MLA in the Alberta Legislature, and an active promoter and booster for the region.

On their second morning at Athabasca Landing, Robert and the rest of his group paddled out in two canoes, heading up the Athabasca River. The Douglas brothers were in one canoe, and Robert, Dr. Sandberg, and an Indigenous guide named Henry were in the other. Robert sat in the bow, the doctor in the middle, and Henry in the stern. The river was smooth and the going was easy. At noon, the group stopped for lunch, dining on bread and butter, canned salmon, tinned pineapple, and a pot of tea. Later, they took an afternoon chocolate break.

While paddling, Robert questioned just what he was doing there. "You damn fool, why are you doing this? You don't have to. You might be lounging in the lobby of a hotel with a cigar and a cocktail, or toying with a tea-cup and chattering to an incendiary blonde. These others are going in on business. They hope to make a fortune. But why are *you* doing it? Just because you have a silly notion in your head that you want to do something with a tang of adventure. Bah! You fake pathfinder, you phony explorer, turn back while there is yet time."

But he resolved to continue—nothing could make him go back. Robert was prepared to risk his life to complete the journey.

The party made camp just before nightfall. After a supper of tinned soup, bacon, jam, and tea, the men retired to their tents. Robert slept in a one-man tent that he could set up in about a minute. It was an oblong sheet of canvas with a rope dividing it, and cords at each corner. He attached one end of the rope to a tree, and the other end to another tree, then pulled tight. The cords were attached to shrubs or roots, and they too were pulled tight. The canvas made a roof, sloping down each side of the central rope, and from the interior dropped a mosquito netting forming a space about seven feet by four. Even when it rained, Robert remained dry and protected from mosquitoes. "I was so happy I did not envy the others their snug sleeping-bags," he later wrote of his sleeping quarters.

The next morning, after a breakfast of bacon, tea, and marmalade, the group resumed their journey. Paddling was effortless, as the river was calm, with no rock obstacles. Near the Athabasca tar sands area, the river widened and the men could see the tar in the river-banks (which made it look like asphalt) and on the water (which made it look like scum). When on the banks, they flung a lit match at the river and the water turned to blue flame.

The group caught up with the Athabasca Brigade on the third day of their journey, around suppertime. The brigade had stopped for the night, camped on the riverbanks near the Grand Rapids. After hoisting their canoes onto a scow and stowing away their gear, the men went ashore and set up their tents. Robert met the flotilla's captain and crew, and chatted with the passengers. Supper was mulligan stew, fried hash, beans, hot biscuits, pie, and coffee.

No longer having to paddle now that they had joined the scows, Robert found the journey "pleasant but boring"—except for some unscheduled canoe action.

This happened the next day, as the brigade neared the Grand Rapids. George Douglas suggested that he and Robert run the rapids in the canoe. "It was a needless bit of bravado," wrote Robert,

Robert Service somewhere between Fort Smith and Fort Norman.
GEORGE MELLIS DOUGLAS COLLECTION / WAYNE DUCHER

"but I felt I must take part. So I sat in the bow as we tackled the tossing river." Robert loosened his bootlaces so that he could get his boots off faster in case he had to swim.

The pair made it safely through the foaming, swirling waters, but inadvertently caused one of the scows to get stuck on a rock. The steersman had become distracted while watching the canoe run the rapids, and had missed seeing the obstacle. George and Robert were then barred from further stunts and antics.

On June 2, the scows reached Fort McMurray, and Robert and the Douglas party transferred to a mosquito-infested stateroom on the 141-foot sternwheeler ss *Grahame*. It would be a week before the steamer would head out on the Athabasca River to Fort Chipewyan and Smith's Landing (renamed Fort Fitzgerald in 1915). So, Robert changed into more casual clothes—slacks and moccasins—and spent the week relaxing and reflecting on how he had fared in the battle of life: "I had gone so low there was no lower, and I had fought my way up. Still in my youth, I need never do another tap of work. I need never think of money, because for every dollar I spent I made two. It seemed fantastic—rags to riches. A knack of romping rhyme had brought me fortune."

On June 9, as the *Grahame* left Fort McMurray, Robert watched as Indigenous and Metis workers started tracking the scows back to Athabasca Landing—it looked like incredibly hard work. The men were harnessed to hauling lines, bringing up the scows one at a time. They heaved, they hauled, and they walked barefoot on the riverbanks.

Three days later, the *Grahame* crossed Lake Athabasca and passed Fort Chipewyan before entering the mouth of the Peace River. It then steamed 160 kilometres upstream to Smith's Landing, where everyone had to disembark and the cargo was unloaded. Ahead was a portage past twenty-five kilometres of rapids on Slave River, including the ominous-sounding Rapids of the Drowned, named for victims of an ill-fated canoe expedition.

At the portage's northern end was the HBC's Fort Smith. The settlement was a gathering place for hardy adventurers as they started their treks to the Barren Lands. And it was here, while waiting for the cargo to be loaded up on the next steamer, that Robert met Harry Radford, a wealthy New Yorker who planned to winter in the interior before crossing the Barren Lands to Hudson Bay.

Radford was known as "Adirondack Harry" in Upstate New York, where he had launched *Woods and Waters*, a popular magazine about hunting and fishing. He said he was travelling to the far north to collect zoological specimens for the Smithsonian Institute and the US Biology Survey. Robert didn't believe him, but rather saw Radford as someone trying to become famous, a brash man who "pushed the idea of exalting himself in his own eyes."

Robert later related an incident that occurred when he and Radford were chatting in a cabin and a small field mouse ran across the floor. Upon spotting the mouse, Radford said, "Let's play football with it," and began to kick it around the room with his feet. When Robert insisted that he stop, Radford looked at him in surprise, insensitive to the animal's suffering.

On the morning of June 27, Radford and his newly hired assistant, George Street (a young Scot from Ottawa, experienced in the wilderness), left Fort Smith to start their journey. They were paddling an 18-foot Peterborough canoe named *Hope*, loaded with a year's worth of supplies. "I think he was scared at the thought of the job he had undertaken ... and as I waved a final farewell, I felt a sudden sympathy for him," noted Robert.

Years later, Robert learned the men were murdered by a group of Inuit at Bathurst Inlet, after Radford had viciously attacked one of the Inuit people. Robert wrote in *Ploughman of the Moon*, "I remembered the mouse and was not surprised. There was something arrogant and tactless in him."

The same day that Radford left Fort Smith, Robert and his companions boarded a 126-foot HBC sternwheeler called the ss *Mackenzie* and began the last leg of their journey to the Arctic. Robert expected it to be a somewhat carefree journey on the Slave River, travelling 565 kilometres through ancient landscapes on their way to Great Slave Lake. But only 50 kilometres upstream, where the Salt River flowed into the Slave, they came upon a grisly murder scene.

Indigenous residents had reported to the Royal North-West Mounted Police (RNWMP) that an unpleasant odour was coming from a trapper's cabin that had been closed for over a month. Robert and the Douglas brothers accompanied the Mounties to the cabin, which sat on a high bluff at the confluence of the Salt and Slave Rivers. When they approached, the stench was overpowering. Robert gagged and shuddered when he learned it was the smell of decaying human flesh.

The sergeant picked up a log and broke the door that had been bolted from the inside. A black cloud of bluebottle flies noisily flew out. Robert peeked into the cabin and saw it was tidy and well kept. Then he saw two men lying dead on the bunk beds. Their decomposing bodies were crawling with maggots and lice, and only their hands and feet were recognizable. A rifle with one discharged shell lay on the floor, and nearby was an empty vial of carbolic acid. The man on the top bunk had been shot in the head at close range; the other man had died gripping his stomach after apparently poisoning himself.

A journal had been kept by one of the men, recording the events of their last days. His words revealed a deteriorating relationship between him and his partner. One entry said he feared his partner, Spud, was going mad, and was going to knife him in the dark while he was sleeping. Another day, he wrote about a fight they'd had over the diary. And then came a dark warning, "Now he wants a chance to kill me. Well I must get him first." The last entry read, "Have killed poor Spud. He was sleeping and would never know. Now I must kill myself. Curse this cruel land! It drives me crazy. God forgive me. Goodbye folks."

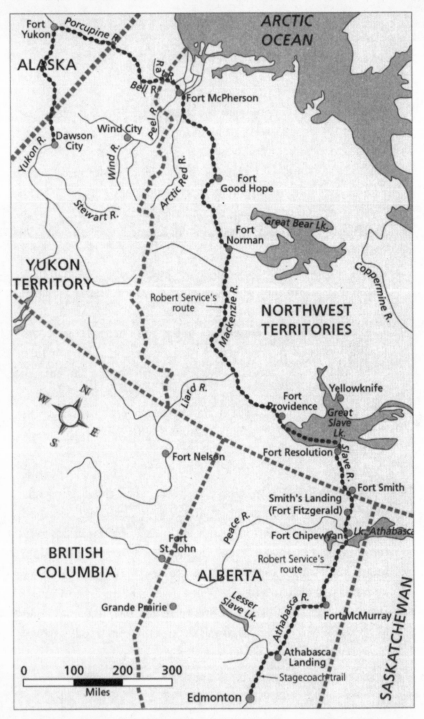

Robert Service's route along the old Edmonton Trail to Dawson City.

The RNWMP sergeant said it was a common story in the North: one trapper goes crazy and kills his partner and then himself. He added that it was tough on the police, though, because they were the ones who had to bury the bodies.

Steaming On The Mackenzie

The ss *Mackenzie* continued on, taking its passengers across Great Slave Lake and up the Mackenzie River, Canada's longest river, flowing over 1600 kilometres to the Beaufort Sea. As the steamer plied the waters, Robert was given advice by seasoned northerners onboard. They warned him about going alone on the journey to Dawson.

"Young man, you're going to your *doom*," said one Indian agent, an ex-parson. A priest with a long silvery beard then cautioned him, "Whatever you do, don't go alone. To travel by oneself in the Arctic is to court death. I know, because I've lived here all my life. A single slip and you are lost."

But Robert was undaunted, and he continued on. By the time the steamer got to Fort Simpson—the oldest settlement on the river—Robert had bought a birchbark canoe for twenty-five dollars from an elderly Indigenous canoe-maker. It was a patchwork of colour: purple, scarlet, primrose, and silver. Its maker had specially selected the bark, sewn it with wood fibre, and lashed it with willow wands. It had taken him a year to make it. Of the sale Robert wrote, "He looked at it with the sadness of an artist who sees his finest work being sold." Robert named his canoe *Coquette*. (The following year, 1912, Robert sent his friends a Christmas picture-postcard of his *Coquette*.)

After Fort Simpson, the ss *Mackenzie* passed the Smoking Hills riverbank, with its perpetually burning seam of coal, then arrived at Fort Norman, a Dene community at the confluence of the Mackenzie and Great Bear Rivers. The community (now called Tulita) was built against Bear Rock Mountain, a tower of limestone that rises over 1500 feet above the water.

The Douglas expedition dropped off at Fort Norman to travel up the Great Bear River to Bear Lake, where they rigged up a sail to their York boat and sailed (along with an Indigenous family) to the eastern end of the lake. Their plan was to overwinter near the abandoned site of Fort Confidence and journey to the Coppermine River the following spring.

Robert continued going up the Mackenzie River with the steamer, stopping next at Fort Good Hope, a Dene community (now called Radeli Ko) established in 1804 as a Roman Catholic mission. A short distance later, Robert crossed the imaginary line of the Arctic Circle and soon after, the mighty Mackenzie River widened to three kilometres across.

The vastness of the Mackenzie Basin impressed Robert, and he developed a deep respect for the people who lived and travelled in it. "There was only a score of them yet they were as well known as if they lived in a village. Stefansson was the uncrowned king of the Arctic, but the others were fearless, hardy, tried, and true. Nearly all met tragic deaths. The Mackenzie was more murderous than the Yukon. Its law was harder, its tribute higher. It killed most of those I knew."

The last HBC post he visited along the Mackenzie was Fort McPherson (now known as Tetlit Zheh, "town of the head waters"). It was here that Robert met one of the North's most hardy men, John Firth, the post manager. Firth had joined the HBC in 1871, arriving on the Mackenzie River the following year. A tall man with clear blue eyes and a white beard, he was born in Orkney, Scotland, in 1854. Firth was a fiddler and a reader, and he was familiar with Robert's books. After selling Robert some supplies, he advised him, "Don't go on. Go back the way you came, like a good little boy."

A RNWMP officer echoed Firth's warning. "Don't you do it. Just think of the Lost Patrol."

The tragedy of the Lost Patrol had occurred earlier in the year, and Robert knew the tale well. It began when four RNWMP officers were sent out on their annual midwinter dogsled patrol between Fort McPherson and Dawson City, a distance of 800 kilometres. Inspector J.E. Fitzgerald was in charge; he had over fourteen years of experience in the frozen North, including serving in the Yukon during the gold rush. Accompanying him were Constables J.F. Kinney and R.O. Taylor, and Special Constable Sam Carter from Dawson City, who was not familiar with the mountainous Richardson Divide they would have to cross. The group had only a rifle, no shot-gun, and were travelling light.

When the patrol set out on December 21, 1910, weather conditions were terrible, with ice fog and heavy snows. Within a week, the men were lost but then, thanks to some travelling Indigenous families, they got back on trail. By January 2, they had travelled a third of the way to Dawson and eaten nearly half of their food. The weather was getting worse. The average temperature was −46 degrees Celsius, with a strong wind that made for a high wind chill. Ten days later, when the group could find no landmarks, they realized they were lost again. With only enough food for nine days, they spent the next seven looking for a trail. On January 18, the food was almost gone, and the men decided to try to head back to Fort McPherson, but the snowstorms had covered their tracks.

Five days later, the temperature was hovering at −53 degrees Celsius and the men were without food. Out of desperation, they turned to their animals for meat, and by February 1, had killed and eaten eight of their fifteen dogs. Fitzgerald's last entry in his journal was written February 5. In that entry, he wrote that only five dogs were left, and that the party was covering only a few kilometres each day. Then, sometime between February 12 and 18, all four men died, three from starvation and one by suicide.

A search party was sent out from Dawson City on February 28, 1911. It included Corporal William John "Jack" Dempster, for whom the Dempster Highway (which runs from Dawson City to Inuvik) was later named. Despite storms and bad weather, they covered the patrol's route in record time. On March 12, they found the frozen bodies of the Lost Patrol only forty-two kilometres from Fort McPherson.

When Robert arrived at Fort McPherson, it had only been four months since the men of the Lost Patrol had been buried there; the memories of the tragedy were fresh in everyone's mind. And it was at Fort McPherson—located where the Peel River joins the Mackenzie River—that Robert would have to decide whether he would return south with the ss *Mackenzie* or go on alone by canoe.

He listened to the warnings from the men of the North, but he chose to go on. After the steamer left, Robert pitched his tent near the Gwich'in encampment, chatted with the chief, and even traded a razor for a walrus ivory fish-hook. Then he put his canoe in the waters of the Peel River and paddled alone towards the Great

Divide—160 kilometres of mountain range that he would have to cross by portaging where he couldn't paddle.

Fate seemed to intervene again. In his autobiography, Robert wrote about meeting up with the scow *Ophelia*, which was heading in the same direction. He joined up with the scow's captain, Captain McTosh, as well as McTosh's wife, and a mate named Jake Skilly. Together, they worked their way down the Peel River for the next few days.

Robert wrote that after they camped at the mouth of the Rat River, they had to pole the fully loaded scow across the Great Divide. Captain McTosh was determined to be the first to cross the Divide with a scow. The group used rope harnesses to tug the *Ophelia* over kilometres of land, often for twelve hours a day and often in knee-deep water. Sometimes the scow had to be unloaded, mounted on runners, and hauled over dry land. Some days, the *Ophelia* travelled only a kilometre. Finally, the group reached a small swampy lake, and after wading and pulling in mud, they made it to the clear waters that would connect them to the Bell River.

At the Bell River, Robert parted company with the *Ophelia* and went on alone, paddling his canoe. He drifted downstream for the next 300 kilometres, hunting game for food. When he reached the Porcupine River, he again met up with the *Ophelia* and hired Jake to paddle with him down the river.

However, by the time they came across a sternwheeler plying the Porcupine River on its way to Dawson City, Robert didn't want to travel with Jake anymore. He had become alarmed at Jake's irrational behaviour and no longer trusted him. Robert hoisted his canoe onboard the sternwheeler and bought passage to Dawson City.

The story goes that while on the sternwheeler, Robert composed his celebrated ballad, *The Ice Worm Cocktail: When the Ice Worms Nest Again*. The squirming ice worms were brought to the public's attention by Stroller White, the editor of the *Whitehorse Star*. Robert taught the ballad to the steamer's crew and they sang it for years.

(There seems to be no record of a Captain McTosh crossing the Great Divide in a scow named *Ophelia*. However, there is a Klondike Gold Rush story about an Albertan named Jim Wallwork, who—with the help of 30 dogs—was the first to haul a scow, *Daisy Belle*, across the Divide in 1898–99. Given Robert's propensity to change names, omit dates, and embellish stories in *Ploughman of the Moon*, one could speculate if there really was an *Ophelia* or a Captain McTosh, or if the tale was cribbed from the story of *Daisy Belle* and Jim Wallwork.)

Back to Dawson City

Dawson City felt good to Robert. He was back in his small cabin with its log steps, overgrown shrubbery, and weathered, handmade lawn chair. Books were piled on the floor. A wicker basket was filled with papers. An old copy of *Outdoor Life* was propped up on a table that was topped with more books.

Robert settled in quickly and started working on his third book of verse, *The Rhymes of a Rolling Stone*, based on his recent adventures in the Mackenzie River Basin and the Arctic. He'd pin rolls of blank wallpaper to his cabin walls and write out his poems with a stick of charcoal in large block letters. Then he'd step back, look at the lines, and make revisions.

74

Robert Service on the porch of his Dawson cabin.
YUKON ARCHIVES, GILLIS FAMILY FONDS 4531

He liked his carefree lifestyle; his time was his own. One of his favourite pastimes was taking long snowshoe hikes along the wilderness trails, and he continued to do this even after one of these walks almost killed him. It was winter and snow covered the ground. Robert decided to visit a friend who lived eighty kilometres away. He walked there and spent a night. The next morning, he set off to return home to his cabin. He walked and walked, but as deep darkness closed in, he realized he had become hopelessly lost in the white wilderness. The temperature dipped to forty below, and the sky was cloudy, so he couldn't use the moon or stars to guide himself home. If he kept going and fell in the snow out of exhaustion, he would likely die.

To get his bearings, Robert walked around a tall pine. Suddenly, the moon broke and he could see a cabin in front of him, only ninety metres away. He staggered to it, but no one was home. He opened the door and lit the stove, ate a bit of food, and collapsed on the bed.

When the owner arrived the next morning, he looked after Robert and persuaded him to stay another night. That night, they drank whiskey. The host became wilder, waved his shotgun around, and told Robert that he was the legendary Cannibal Joe, who supposedly killed and then ate his partner (the two of them had been prospecting in the Barren Lands and ran out of food).

As the night went on, the atmosphere in the cabin grew terrifying. Cannibal Joe insisted on telling Robert his side of the story: his partner's dying words had been to tell Joe to save himself by using his corpse. But Joe said, "I never ate Bob. I never ate a single slice of him. Ne, that's not what I want to tell you... What did I do? Listen—God curse me! I never et Bo, but *I fed him to the dogs and I et the bloody dogs.*" Then Cannibal Joe passed out on the floor.

The next morning, Cannibal Joe made bacon and eggs for Robert and chatted amiably. As Robert left, Joe's parting words were "say friend, if ye had a bad dream last night ye just want to ferget it. Yundersand?"

Robert finished writing *Rhymes of a Rolling Stone* in the spring of 1912. The manuscript ran to 120 pages, with 51 pieces. He stayed the summer, then left Dawson City on the last steamer of the season headed to Vancouver. It would be the last time he was ever in the Yukon.

By September, Robert was in Toronto before heading to New York to deliver the manuscript to his publishers. His plan was to winter in the South Seas—royalties were still providing a good income, and he didn't have to work. However, his plans changed when the *Toronto Star* asked him to cover the Balkan War as their war correspondent. Unable to turn down such an exciting offer, he crossed the Atlantic Ocean on the *Victoria Luise* (formerly the *Deutschland*), an ocean cruise liner from the Hamburg America Line that carried over 1100 passengers.

The Bard of the Yukon and Poet of the Mackenzie would soon become the Poet of the War Ballads.

CHAPTER

5

Poet of
the First World War

THE BALKAN WAR lasted from October 17 to December 3, 1912. It began when the Balkan League (Serbia, Bulgaria, Greece, and Montenegro) declared war on the crumbling Ottoman Empire. They attacked Turkey, conquered its European territories, and left it the small area it has now.

When Robert arrived in Istanbul, the authorities wouldn't give him permission to get to the front lines. He volunteered for the Turkish Red Crescent to get closer to the action, and though he still didn't get to the actual fighting, he did get to see the ugly side of war. As a volunteer, he delivered rice to a cholera camp in San Stefano. He carried corpses out of a hospital that had once been a luxury Turkish resort. And he worked in a camp where thousands of tents had been set up for the wounded soldiers. He was appalled at the misery and the suffering.

However, when the colonel-in-charge found out that Robert worked for a newspaper, he dismissed him. Robert went back to Istanbul, ready to join other reporters attempting to get to the front lines, but a visit from two plainclothesmen changed his plans. They checked his documents and ordered him to report to the Commissariat of Police in Istanbul the next day at 3 PM It sounded threatening, and rather than put himself in possible danger, he quickly booked passage to leave on the first ship the next morning. All night he worried about being arrested before he could flee, but in the morning, he boarded a Romanian steamer and sailed away on the Black Sea.

The wanderlust kept him moving and wandering through eastern and central Europe. He travelled on the Orient Express, stayed in opulent hotels, like Bucharest's Palace Hotel, and in cheap ones, like Sacher's Hotel in Vienna.

Robert arrived in Paris in March of 1913—and felt he had come home. He lived in modest rooms on the Quai Voltaire, attended art classes, and walked the city.

He also began to move in the literary circles of the time, mingling with prominent international correspondents, journalists, poets, novelists, and humorists. Paris would be home to Robert for the next 15 years, and it would be featured in his writings.

At loose ends again, Robert put his life in fate's hands. What would he do next? Who would he meet? It wasn't long before he started on his next adventure—a romantic one that lasted the rest of his life.

The Adventure of Lifelong Love

It was the spring of 1913 when Robert met a woman named Germaine during a military parade in Paris. She and her sister, Helen, were literally being swept away by the crowd. He went to their rescue, and soon the chance encounter became a romance. Germaine was the youngest daughter of Marie Emélie Klein and Constant Bourgain, a distillery owner.

In his autobiography, Robert wrote, "I wanted a home, a settled life, respectability, convention. I viewed the Quarter with growing disgust. A bunch of lousy libertines laughing all the day long! I had had enough of that. I was due to play a new part."

He didn't tell Germaine that he was a successful poet, but one of Germaine's girlfriends had recognized Robert's name and told her he was the famous poet who had written *The Cremation of Sam McGee*.

The couple married on June 12, 1913, in Paris. Germaine recalled that after the wedding, they went to London for a week, then took a steamer back to France and bike-toured in St. Malo, looking for a small holiday home. In August, they found their dream home near Lancieux, Brittany. Owned by the town's mayor, it was a small, red-roofed cottage that stood on a rock jutting into the sea. They purchased it through a real estate agent, and named their new summer residence, Dream Haven. (In *Ploughman of the Moon*, Robert somewhat embellished the purchase of Dream Haven, and his memory of the event differs from Germaine's. He claimed that he had tricked the town's mayor into selling him the house at a discount price, before he met Germaine.)

The Services would summer at Dream Haven and winter in Paris. Their first Paris home was a Spartan, two-room apartment just off Boulevard Raspail. Germaine made all the curtains and cushions, and Robert wrote his novel, *The Pretender: A Story of the Latin Quarter* (a melodrama about the literary circles in Paris, London, and New York). Published in 1914, the critics didn't like the book, saying they expected something better from Service.

He also wrote a six-week series, *Zig-Zags of a Vagabond*, that the *Toronto Star* ran from December 6, 1913, to January 10, 1914. With titles like "Paris, City of Alienating Seduction," "Montmartre, the Monstrosity," and "Afoot in Fontainebleau," the articles were so popular that the newspaper clamoured for more. Readers loved the upbeat tone of the articles, and Robert enjoyed writing them. "It was easy to write those articles for I was so supremely happy... Little things that others took for granted—my morning croissant and coffee on the terrace, my reflective pipe, my lonely walk along the Seine, evenings under the trees in the purple twilight—all of these were to me sources of divine content... Again I discovered the rich satisfaction of creative effort," he said. "I was so happy it almost hurt."

But Robert felt it was all too good to last: "Something sinister is beneath it all." And he was right. One day, while he was walking along a field with Germaine, he heard the village church bells ringing. Down the path, a neighbour was running and crying out, "War. Our men will have to go..."

It was August 1914 when the First World War began. Later, Robert would write, "Never again would we see that eager, careless world."

First World War

Robert tried to enlist in the war, but was rejected on medical grounds (he had a varicose vein in his left calf). He'd wanted to join the Seaforths Battalion, a battalion that was later annihilated on the Somme. (Over 20,000 British died on July 1, 1916, the first day of the Battle of the Somme.)

Unhappy that he couldn't be part of the war effort, Robert stayed in Paris, waiting to see where destiny would take him next. In January 1915, he attended a Robert Burns dinner organized by the expatriate British community. The speaker was John Buchan, author of 16 books including *The Thirty-Nine Steps*. When the two men spoke at dinner, Buchan rekindled Robert's adventuring spirit by encouraging him to look at other ways to join the war effort. (Buchan later became Lord Tweedsmuir and the Governor General of Canada).

Robert rejoined the *Toronto Star* as their war correspondent and headed north to Calais, where he would be closer to the main British base camp. He stayed at the Station Hotel with other journalists, but was surprised to learn that their news reporting relied on stories from front-line soldiers, rather than digging for first-hand material. The journalists warned Robert to stay away from Dunkirk if he valued his life, but they didn't realize their advice would only motivate him to do the opposite. Dunkirk, on the North Sea, was only seventeen kilometres from the Belgian border, close to the front line of the war.

Robert took a train to a village near Dunkirk and once there, stopped in a cafe for coffee. When he noticed the landlord making a hasty call, he knew he was in danger and left quickly. He walked to Dunkirk and headed for the town centre. All day, he wandered freely through the city, priding himself on getting there ahead of the other journalists, and confident he had a scoop story.

That evening, he was arrested as a spy by a French gendarme and brought to a major who examined his passport, noting the visa stamps from Turkey, Bulgaria, Austria, and Germany. Robert was marched through the streets of Dunkirk, hissed at by an angry French mob, and locked in a guardroom overnight.

The next day, he was brought to see a commanding British officer and ordered out of town after a severe reprimand. Robert was told that Dunkirk was crawling with rumours of spies, and that the French had already shot some spy suspects. Back in Calais, he thought his escape would impress the journalists, but they simply laughed.

Robert wanted to get to where the real war action was taking place, so he joined the American Ambulance Unit as a volunteer ambulance driver. The unit, started by American expatriates in Paris, was attached to the French army.

A number of famous authors became ambulance drivers during the First World War—well known literary figures like Ernest Hemingway, e. e. cummings, Charles Nordhoff, John Dos Passos, John Masefield, William Seabrook, and Somerset Maugham.

The ambulance drivers were known as "gentlemen drivers," and enjoyed officer status, but some, like Robert, didn't like their noncombatant role: "I did not wear my Red Cross arm band, for I was ashamed I was not a combatant. Though I did not want to kill I was willing to take a chance of being killed. If only I could get some gore on my uniform, I might feel better."

Robert was soon driving an ambulance under enemy gunfire. In June 1915, at Neuville St. Vaast, the French army launched a furious assault on the German lines, and Robert's unit was working in the vicinity. He later wrote about the scene: "It was on a long stretch of Flanders road, and I had five wounded in my car. This road was raked by a German battery as I hurried over it. Suddenly

I heard a shell burst. I saw a cloud of black smoke, while gravel and stones spattered the car. I hesitated to dash in or to stop; but my orders had been to do the latter, so I put on the brakes. A good job too, for ahead there was another explosion with a mushroom of evil black smoke. I had three walking wounded and two stretcher cases, so with the aid of the first, I got the stretchers into the ditch and there we waited till dusk. I had felt no fear, only a thrill that I had something of pleasure in it. I had been under fire. I could go back to Chelsea now and take a salute."

Despite this short bit of action, Robert compared his job to driving a taxi, not being a soldier. He craved more excitement, something that would bring him right to the fighting lines.

He got his opportunity when he was assigned to outpost duty—ambulance posts close to the first aid stations, with cars ready round the clock. Two drivers were assigned to each car for ten-day shifts. They slept in their clothes, dozing in ruined cottages, tents, or dugouts, and were constantly exposed to shellfire. The ambulance drivers drove through rain, hail, mud, and dust. Heads thrust over the steering wheel, eyes staring intently ahead, they'd drive beside a trench or dugout to pick up a wounded soldier, and then creep along back out.

Night driving without lights on unfamiliar shell-pitted roads was the worst, and Robert later wrote, "It was nerve-wracking, crawling on low speed, with a badly wounded man along those coal-black devastated roads." Robert also took a position as a stretcher-bearer, heading directly into the firing trenches.

These hazards gave him and his companions a pride in their job, but it was also emotionally taxing to listen to men going mad with pain, see the young become quickly toughened, and watch the glow of a burning town. Most of the British volunteers were Robert's age, while the younger men were Americans, whose country was still neutral.

One of the most hair-raising trips, which Robert performed regularly, was along a roadway called the Sacred Way. Only six metres wide, the Sacred Way ran along the track of an abandoned railway and, despite constant artillery attack, was used to maintain contact with the French front line at Verdun. Every division of the French army had passed over this road on their way to the front line; and now, an armada of over 10,000 motor vehicles in unbroken lines travelled along it day and night to service the French army. In one 24-hour period in February 1916, no fewer than 6,000 vehicles passed along this narrow lane—one every fourteen seconds. They travelled at eighteen kilometres an hour at a distance of sixty feet from one another, as ambulances weaved by. Danger was ever present, but there was still a camaraderie among the men of the Ambulance Corps, one that reminded Robert of his bank group in Dawson City.

In June 1916, Robert had to go on medical leave because of recurring boils. His condition had started months earlier, when one day he'd noticed a tiny black speck on his leg that looked like an insect bite. The next day, the area was swollen. It was the beginning of a long bout with boils; sometimes he had three or four, sometimes simply one big one. Over a period of eight months, he counted 99 boils (he was waiting for the 100th one, as he liked round numbers). Robert returned to Paris, and then headed to Dream Haven with Germaine to recover. The boils continued for a time, then suddenly disappeared.

While convalescing, he put his ambulance driver experiences to verse. He had not kept a diary, but the memories were clear in his mind. The brave soldiers of the First World War became the people of his ballads in *Rhymes of a Red Cross Man*; they replaced the rugged jovial characters of the Canadian North.

After five months, *Rhymes of a Red Cross Man* was ready for print. Published in late 1916, the book contained fifty-three war ballads and stayed on the bestseller list for the next nine months. (*Rhymes of a Red Cross Man* was also used over fifty years later in the trauma clinics for returning Vietnam veterans.)

This book of verse was different than his others. Before, he had written verse as the observer, but in *Rhymes of a Red Cross Man* he spoke from experiencing first-hand the devastation of war. He had seen and lived the horror.

Author James Mackay comments on Robert's book in *Vagabond of Verse*: "Readers were confronted with vivid sensations of soldiers marching gaily 'up the line' and their rapid sense of shock and disillusions when coming under the withering hail of machine-guns or the incessant bombardment of artillery. There is a gut-wrenching wait of the signal to go 'over the top'... There is the pain and the suffering, the nostalgia for home and loved ones, and the longing not for victory but merely an end to it all. Gone are the absurdities of Dan McGrew and Sam McGee. Here is the anguish of a sensitive writer who had been through it all..."

And just as there had been with his Boer War verses, Robert had a personal connection with this war: his brother Albert was killed in action in France. Robert dedicated *Rhymes of a Red Cross Man*, "To the Memory of My Brother LIEUTENANT ALBERT SERVICE Canadian Infantry Killed in Action. France, August 1916."

Amidst the business of war, there was a wonderful event in Robert's life. He and Germaine became parents to twin girls, Doris and Iris, on January 28, 1917. Robert thoroughly enjoyed his new role as a father, and wasn't disappointed when the ambulance corps was disbanded later that year.

Paris was becoming dangerous, so the Services took their daughters with them to winter in the Riviera. It was here that tragedy struck. Their daughter Doris caught scarlet fever and died on February 25, 1918, at thirteen months old. Robert was devastated. To a friend, he wrote that he would cry whenever he thought of the loss of his beloved daughter.

The Services then returned to Dream Haven in Lancieux. Once again feeling guilty about not contributing to the war, Robert offered his services to the Canadian government, and in the spring of 1918 was assigned to the Canadian Expeditionary Force (CEF). His duty would be to report on the activities of the Canadian troops in France.

Robert was provided with a chauffeured Cadillac, an officer guide, and freedom to plan his own itinerary. He toured the Canadian army camps and inspected airfields, hospitals, field kitchens, and ordnance depots. He visited the Canadian infantry and artillery on the front line. And he made a personal pilgrimage to the grave of his brother Albert, who was buried in a corner of the Ypres Salient.

On a visit to the 8th Battalion CEF, he met up again with a familiar face from the Canadian North: Jim "Peace River" Cornwall, who was commander of the battalion. Together, they toured a recent battlefront in southern Belgium, where there were still German bodies lying everywhere.

Near the end of the war, Robert met another Canadian icon of the North: Joe "King of the Klondike" Boyle. At the beginning of the war, Boyle had outfitted a company of Yukon northerners for active war service in Europe. As Colonel Boyle DSO OBE, he headed an Allied military mission to Romania and saved that country from annihilation. He became a close friend of the Romanian royal family and introduced them to Robert's poetry. When Boyle died in 1923, Romania's Queen Marie paid for his tombstone, on which she inscribed Robert's words from the *Law of the Yukon*:

> *A man with the heart of a Viking*
> *And the simple faith of a child.*

Robert visited Le Cateau after it was attacked with mustard gas. He went through a village where every house had been looted, vandalized, and destroyed. He saw a battlefield that he compared to a charnel house: "Heaps of bodies littered the ground… Dead, dead everywhere—so many of them. One hoped they would be buried before they had time to putrefy. But the burial parties were working night and day…"

In the fall of 1918, Robert accompanied a Canadian major as they drove, unknowingly, beyond the Allied front lines and through seemingly deserted villages where people suddenly appeared, joyful to see them. They drove on until they reached the outskirts of Lille, a town in northern France near the Belgian border that was thought to still be in enemy hands. But there were no signs of the Germans, so they entered the city by the Cambrai gates and walked ahead on foot to the cheering crowds, while Germans were retreating on the other side of the city. The mayor invited them to the town hall, and Robert made a speech in French,

Robert Service, carrying a bouquet of flowers, giving an
uofficial liberation speech in Lille, France, October 1918.
QUEEN'S UNIVERSITY ARCHIVES

but when they spotted a staff car of German top brass heading
their way, they quickly escaped.

Once he was back in Paris, Robert worked feverishly to produce
a book called *War Winners*, recognizing those who often received
no recognition or glory in victory. As he was working on the book,
the war was declared over. He celebrated all day. But later, he was
overwhelmed by intense hatred for war and its pain and suffering.
He picked up the manuscript and passionately tore it up. "No more
war... Curse the memory of it," he later wrote.

For his war service, Robert received the three standard war med-
als: The 1914–15 Star, the British War Medal, and the Victory Medal.

6

The Travelling
Poet

BACK IN PARIS in the spring of 1919, the Services moved to a new ten-room, two-storey apartment. The upper floor became Robert's studio and library.

He started work on his fifth volume of verse, *Ballads of a Bohemian*, trying something new in its creation. He split the book into four sections, one for each season, and he linked his verses with paragraphs of prose. The book was finished on December 19, but he simply put it away, saying he was "sick of the literary game" and that "poetry was a disease." He wanted to concentrate now on writing novels. *Ballads of a Bohemian* was finally published in 1921. It would be another nineteen years before Robert would publish verse again.

California Calls

A movie deal for *The Shooting of Dan McGrew* enticed Robert back to Hollywood in the autumn of 1921, over twenty years after he had left. He became fascinated with the film world, visiting the movie studios and forming friendships with big stars like Noah Berry and William "Big Bill" Russell.

The Services settled into Hollywood life, renting a small bungalow for six months. Robert's mother Emily, now living in Edmonton, joined them for Christmas and then stayed until May. She met her daughter-in-law Germaine and granddaughter Iris for the first time.

Emily took the Oregon Express train to Hollywood, and when Robert went to pick her up, he was worried he wouldn't recognize her after all this time. And he didn't—he mistook two other women for his mother before spotting Emily.

It was a tranquil period in Robert's life. The family would eat out for lunch and stay home for dinner. He was a wealthy man now, but the Scot in Robert kept him frugal. On his daily walks, he would gather empty wooden crates discarded by shopkeepers and use them as firewood in their fireplace.

Emily got along well with Germaine and Iris. Robert was pleased that everyone seemed so happy because he was restless and anxious to go travelling again. He wanted to go to the South Pacific, and he wanted to go alone.

Without any prior discussion, he asked his family if they would mind if he left for about two months while they stayed behind in Hollywood. He gave the argument that every novelist had to write a romance about the South Seas, and had to travel there first to get the feel of the place. The room went silent. No one spoke a word. Finally, his mother simply said, "Go." Germaine later commented that his sudden decision came just after Iris's fifth birthday in January.

Three days later, Robert boarded the ss *Rarotonga*, bound for Tahiti (which was called French Oceania at the time). The wanderlust poet was on the move again, charged with the "spirit of adventure and romance." And once more, he was following the footsteps of his literary hero, Robert Louis Stevenson.

Time Out in Tahiti

In Tahiti, Robert rented a bungalow with a balcony, relaxed on a hammock, and enjoyed his solitude. When life became too routine, he took a week to walk around the island. People treated him with kindness, sometimes preparing meals for him, other times offering their homes for a night's accommodation. He was impressed with the good manners and courtesy of the islanders. At some point, he stumbled upon a leper colony. He asked one British man with leprosy if he could do anything for him. According to Robert, the man answered, in a high society British voice, that there was nothing he could do because, "I'm dead, officially dead. Goodbye."

While still in Tahiti, Robert reunited with two fellow ambulance drivers from the war, authors Charles Bernard Nordhoff and James Norman Hall. The two would later gain international recognition for writing *Mutiny on the Bounty*. Robert also visited "Major Brandish," another ambulance driver who now owned a vanilla plantation on the island.

After he had been there a while, Robert decided to leave Tahiti and visit the island of Moorea. Since there were no inter-island ferries in 1922, he hired an old fisherman, who insisted they leave at sunset to get the full advantage of a good wind. It was a harrowing ninety-minute journey because the boat owner was drunk. He ploughed through gigantic combers that crashed on the coral reef (which circled the island 200 metres from shore). Then the boat itself crashed into the reef, making a frightening grinding sound. The two passengers made it to the smooth inland waters, but as they entered Moorea's bay, the waters became so choppy that Robert became violently seasick before landing.

After passing two months in the South Seas, he sailed back to Los Angeles to join his family, who were still living in their Hollywood apartment. When their lease expired in May 1922, Robert's mother returned to Edmonton and the Services went back to Paris.

Robert wrote nostalgically about watching his mother leave on the train to Alberta: "She glided from the scene like a princess with her black dress. Her gold chain and her cameo broach, she took with her an atmosphere almost Victorian." Emily was a feisty woman, with bright blue eyes and a laughing smile. She liked to play solitaire, eat ice cream, watch gangster films, and read crime detective fiction. She wished that Robert would write a crime story, and he vowed that he would someday fulfil her wish.

Back in Paris, Robert settled down to a comfortable routine of taking his daughter to school each morning and later, enjoying her stories about the day. For the next seven years, his priorities centred on his family. He wrote to a friend in Canada, "I don't write much with enthusiasm these days. Getting old, I suppose; and I have enough money to live on nicely without working. However, if I gave up entirely I should be bored, as I cannot develop any hobbies. I do not think I will ever again visit Canada. When I think of Dawson and all that life it seems like a dream. I used to consider myself a bit of an authority on the Yukon, but now my ignorance is abysmal."

His focus was now on writing novels, not verse. In 1922, he finished *The Poisoned Paradise*, a novel about gambling techniques he had observed in Monte Carlo. The book was well received and the movie rights sold quickly. It would later become a box office hit starring Clara Bow.

In 1922, he also worked on a new novel, *The Roughneck*, based on his travels in Tahiti. The plot was far-fetched and the characters shallow, but the public loved it. It was published a year later, and in 1924 was made into a movie—the third of his novels to make it into film.

The Health Guru

In January 1924, Robert celebrated his fiftieth birthday and embarked on a new adventure, one that could be much more deadly than anything he had tackled before.

Robert expected to hear good news after going for his annual physical. He looked a picture of health, having the physique of someone much younger. And every day, he worked out in the gym for two hours, swam before lunch, and hiked in the afternoon. Therefore, he was shocked when the doctor told him he would be dead in another ten years unless he slowed down and changed his lifestyle.

Apparently, Robert was in bad shape. He had a defective heart, hypertrophy, and abnormally high blood pressure, at times hitting over 200. Robert was told to give up alcohol, tobacco, red meat, and coffee, to eat very little in the evening, and to continue walking, but never to hurry. Obsessed with his heart condition,

Robert became a hypochondriac. He had panic attacks. He consulted other doctors but they all confirmed the diagnosis.

For the next year, his health became his work. He became such an advocate of healthy living that he wrote what he believed was the most meaningful book in his career: *Why Not Grow Young? Keeping Fit at Fifty*. Published in 1928, it was a philosophical self-help book with advice for healthy living. The book didn't sell well. Disappointed, Robert commented: "From Yukon ballad to health homilies was too rude a break even for my most devoted fans."

Feeling resigned to having to live at a slower pace, he wrote in a March letter to Charles Gibbons (who was now an editor in Vancouver), "I have reverted to type and am now the conventional middle-aged Englishman with urban ideas and the aspiration to be fully civilized. A touch of heart trouble due to an effort to write a book on physical culture and pose for my own illustrations has helped to tame me and reconcile me to a life of comparative culture and refinement. In short, my days of action, with their memories of North and West, are over and I accept the tranquilly speculative years."

He slowed down his pace of living but continued work on his two unfinished novels. *The Master of the Microbe* was published in 1926, and *The House of Fear* in 1927. The latter book, dedicated to his mother, would be the last novel that Robert would ever write.

In 1929, Robert faced a new challenge in his career: he learned he was being sued for 10,000 pounds. He wrote in his memoirs: "Up to now lawyers had played no part in my existence and I disliked them as much as I did doctors. And now this letter left me paralysed with horror. With heart thumping I read it over and over, scarce believing my eyes. For it accused me of libel most foul and reptilian."

It seemed an English peer felt Robert had insulted an ancestor in one of his books. By all accounts, the grounds for libel were weak, but Robert feared the legal process and, without consulting a lawyer, agreed to pay the demanded 10,000 pounds. "It was not the money that mattered but the horror of appearing in court," he later wrote. His friend H.G. Wells had recommended he fight the libel suit, noting, "Writing is becoming one of the dangerous occupations."

In autumn of 1929, the Services returned to the Riviera, renting a ten-room apartment in the working class section of Nice. Robert had a huge area to himself, consisting of his bedroom, a den, a workroom, and a library (his guitar collection was displayed on the wall above the books). Life was good; he and the family wintered in the warm, sunny Riviera and summered in Lancieux at Dream Haven.

Robert did a little writing, but mostly played guitar, accordion, and piano. He wrote songs for the guitar, later arranging them for the piano. As a songwriter, he put his best twenty songs in a book called *Twenty Bath-Tub Ballads* and sent it to a publisher.

His life revolved around long walks, physical culture, and music making. He was so laid back at this stage that even reading his own obituary in the newspaper didn't alarm him. The article was about poets killed in the First World War. The media picked up the story, announcing the "Bard of the Yukon" was dead. Robert was amused and didn't bother to correct the announcement. Even his own brothers thought he had passed away.

The slow-paced dream life in Europe, however, was beginning to crack and would soon shatter. France became unstable, with riots and strikes. There was a financial crisis, with the French franc being devalued, and in the summer of 1938, things swung to the right in France, producing a communist backlash. The same year, civil war broke out in neighbouring Spain

The continuing instability got Robert's attention. Wanting to hear from both sides of the political spectrum, he read the papers and attended the political meetings of both the communists and the fascists. Once, he even joined the crowd outside a newspaper office and watched the smashing of windows and property destruction.

The fiery political atmosphere prompted him to go on a new adventure: visiting Russia and seeing firsthand what communism was about. He booked a tour with Intourist (the travel agency of the Soviet government) and left for Russia in July, 1938.

The Russian Adventures

The Russia of the late 1930s was a brutal communist country headed by dictator Joseph Stalin. It had a secretive government, where information was controlled by the state and mixed with state propaganda. It was the job of the Intourist guides to ensure outsiders didn't see the real Russia.

Robert could see through the propaganda; he observed the seediness, the poverty, and the dilapidated conditions. But he enjoyed meeting the people, noting, "I like Russians, but I disliked Communists." An American, a former communist supporter, approached Robert's tour group and asked them to take a message out of Russia to his family. The man said he couldn't leave the country and begged the group to help save his life. But none of the group assisted, wary they were being tricked by the Soviet secret police.

The next day, by coincidence, the police confined the tour group to their hotel due to an investigation, and prevented them from leaving Moscow. Robert wanted to leave right away, but all the group members were denied train tickets. When tickets were suddenly available, they rushed to catch the train to get out of Russia.

The frightening plans of both the Soviets and the Germans were beginning to surface. Armed Soviet guards searched the undercarriages of the trains Robert rode, looking for their "escaping" citizens. And in Germany, Robert watched as Nazi soldiers removed from his compartment a young Jewish man sitting across from him. Later he learned the man had been taken to the interrogation room, stripped, and examined for concealed jewels.

Two months after he left for Russia, Robert was back in Paris, and the Services were soon off to winter in Nice. It was the fall of 1938, and Robert started work on his new novel, *Four Blind Mice*, an escape story set in Russia. After typing 10,000 words, he suddenly stopped and realized he didn't have enough knowledge about the country. To finish the book, he felt he had to return to Russia for more research.

In July 1939, almost exactly a year after his first trip, Robert left Paris on a train headed for Russia. His route would take him through Germany and Poland. Along the way, he noticed that German military uniforms were everywhere, and that people, even children, were fervently shouting "Heil Hitler!"

As he was leaving Germany, he experienced German militarism first-hand when he had to face an angry Nazi customs official at the border. The official ordered Robert to go to the interrogation cell under the railway station. There, a young German took over and started to question him aggressively. Robert was convinced he was now in the hands of the dreaded Gestapo. The man searched his luggage, and when he found a book by Jewish writer Max Nardau, he demanded to know why Robert had a copy. Robert later wrote, "In that bare vault the air was charged with hostility." To his relief, the Nazi official finally released Robert and allowed him to continue his train trip to Russia.

Robert stayed two weeks in Moscow, cruised down the Volga, and travelled through Stalingrad, Georgia, the Black Sea, and Yalta. Near the end of his journey, he sensed the tides of war were swelling. He was in Odessa when he heard that on August 23, the Soviets and Germans had signed a secret protocol that included dividing Poland between them. A day later, when Robert arrived in Kiev, he felt he was being watched by the Soviet secret police. He decided to return home immediately. After some tense negotiations for a train ticket, he left Kiev for Warsaw, and from there, planned to continue by train through Germany to Paris. But life was no longer simple. On August 25, as a last strategy to stop an imminent German attack on Poland, Great Britain announced an alliance with Poland. Tensions were building towards a full war.

On September 1, 1939, after reaching the Polish border, Robert changed trains to continue his trip to Warsaw. But before the train departed, a Polish officer came onboard and announced that the German border was now closed, and that Poland was at war with Germany. Robert made it safely to Warsaw and was there when the first wave of German attacks began.

The British Consul met Robert at the Warsaw train terminus and advised him to leave Poland on the evening train going north to Tallinn, Estonia. From there, Robert could take a Baltic steamer to Stockholm, train it to Bergen (Norway), and board a ship to Newcastle, England. After reaching England, he could take another train to London and then head for France. It would be a roundabout way to get home, but there was no other option.

The crowded night train had an air of impending danger. First it passed through the Polish city of Wilno (now Vilnius, Lithuania); two weeks later, on October 10, 1939, the city would be seized by Soviet troops. The next day, when they arrived in Tallinn, Robert had to wait hours at the dock for their steamer.

It was a dark time in Estonia. The Soviets wanted to control the small but geographically strategic nation. Estonian culture was one of the oldest in Europe, its people had been there for over 5,000 years. Soon it would be brutally occupied by the Soviets. Robert called Tallinn a city "whose bleakness matched my own mood."

Robert got to Bergen and boarded a ship to cross the North Sea to England. It would be a dangerous trip—German submarines were cruising the North Sea, ready to attack. His ship, the ss *Venus*, made some detours and got safely to Newcastle. (Within a year, the ss *Venus* was seized by Germany on this route and in 1945, the ship sank after being bombed.)

But Robert's troubles were not over: France had suspended his visa and he was now stuck in London, a city preparing for war. Most people carried gas masks. Sandbags were piled in front of shops. Windows were crossed with tape. Robert wrote and told Germaine to go to their winter home in Nice and to guard his manuscript of verse.

Three weeks later, with his visa in hand, he left Britain. At the border all his books were confiscated, except for his Russian diary.

Then, when he arrived in Paris, the authorities told him that Nice was now a war zone and that travel was strictly forbidden. He ignored the warning and took a train to Nice to be with his family.

It was a strange time in Europe. In September 1939, a number of countries had declared war on Germany, including Britain, France, Australia, New Zealand, South Africa, and Canada. Yet no one was fighting. Historians have dubbed this period the Phoney War. For seven months, the Phoney War continued. Countries were threatening war while talking peace. Regardless of the rhetoric, there was a sense of impending disaster.

In the meantime, the Services were wintering in Nice and life was fairly routine. In the spring of 1940, Robert published *Bar-Room Ballads*, his first book of verse in nineteen years. It was 120 pages, with forty-six pieces and five "frivolous" songs. A diverse mix of work, it included *The Ballad of Lenin's Tomb, Tahiti Days*, and *Warsaw*.

About the same time, Robert heard that Italian leader Benito Mussolini was threatening to annex Nice to Italy. The front lines of the war were getting a little too close, and Robert decided to return early to the family's home at Lancieux. He was almost too late—the German Blitzkrieg started on May 10, 1940.

Quickly, Robert got his family back to Lancieux, only to find that the village was crowded with war refugees. They heard grim stories of Germans advancement and destruction. Food was becoming scarce in the village. More refugees arrived, some now from Paris. The Germans were advancing on France.

On June 4, 1940, the last ships departed the beaches of Dunkirk, rescuing the last of the 340,000 British, French, Belgium, and Dutch Allied forces, and civilians from North France.

On June 13, the first German bombs hit Lancieux, in a field close to Dream Haven. Germaine and Iris wanted to flee immediately, but Robert held firm, insisting he wasn't going to leave. He wanted to see how the war was going to play out in France. Finally, for his family's sake, he agreed to flee.

Four days later, on the afternoon of June 17, he went for a ride on his motorbike to assess the situation. People along the road warned him that there were Germans ahead, but Robert wanted to see for himself before fleeing. He hid in a roadside haystack as a stream of Germans drove by, a "swift stream of motorcycles by green-helmeted and goggled warriors armed to the teeth." Quickly, Robert rode to the seaport of Saint-Malo and saw four British steamers evacuating wounded British troops. Wanting to escape the coming mayhem, he asked if he and his family could get passage to England. There was a chance, he was told, if he was there before the steamers set sail.

He returned to Lancieux and ordered Germaine and Iris to quickly get ready to leave. "We're going... you can only take one suitcase each and I give you half-an-hour to pack." While waiting, Robert burned his banking papers and said farewell to Dream Haven, the home he loved. The three then drove the back lanes to get to Saint-Malo.

Along the way, they passed lines of bullet-riddled cars coming from neighbouring Renne—cars with broken windows and filled with injured passengers. The Germans had heavily bombed Renne, killing over 2,000 people in one day.

That evening, the Services boarded an old coal-carrier steamer called *Hull Trader* that was being used in the war's Operation Aerial to evacuate British soldiers and civilians. Shortly before the steamer left Saint-Malo, another group of injured soldiers was boarded. The ship now carried 500 troops, 50 refugees (like the Services), and several hundred wounded.

At sunset with a full moon, the *Hull Trader*, along with two other evacuation ships, steamed out of Saint-Malo. All three ships were headed for Weymouth in England. The Royal Air Force provided fighter cover to minimize the chances of enemy aircraft bombing, but hitting a mine or being attacked by enemy submarines was on everyone's mind.

Robert knew their voyage was a dangerous one. "That water was just staked with disaster and every moment of that night I lay awake awaiting the shock of being hurled to eternity," he wrote in his memoirs.

The *Hull Trader* arrived safely the next day in England. But a year later, the ship was destroyed—and eleven of her fourteen crew were killed—when she hit a mine while hauling cargo between London and Hull.

The Services had made it to England and, after medical checkups, delousing, police interrogation (twice), and a journey under armed guard to London, they were given hot baths, their passports were stamped, and they were released.

But their stay in London would be short-lived—within two months they would be sailing again.

CHAPTER

7

The World War II Years

THE INTENSE BOMBING raids on London began on August 24, 1940. Two weeks later, the London apartment where the Services had been living was destroyed. Fortunately, they were no longer there; they had already fled England.

The family left England on July 26 onboard the *Princess Helene*, a 4,000-ton Canadian Pacific steamship headed for Montreal. The steamer normally sailed between Saint John, New Brunswick and Digby, Nova Scotia, but when war was declared by Canada in 1939, Canadian Pacific had offered all its ships for the war effort. Some, like the *Princess Helene*, were converted into troopships. Along with the Services, the *Princess Helene* was carrying over 1,000 evacuated children and a contingent of Royal Air Force cadets travelling to Alberta for flight training.

The first three days crossing the Atlantic were harrowing. The *Princess Helene* and its destroyer escort dodged enemy submarines, and lifejackets were worn by everyone at all times, day and night. On the fourth day, the destroyer headed back to England having escorted the *Princess Helene* to a safe zone.

The media were waiting for Robert when they arrived in Montreal on August 1. Reporters clamoured to talk to the famous poet, eager to get his comments on escaping from France. His return to Canada unleashed frenzied media activity—perfect publicity for the Canadian edition of *Bar-Room Ballads*.

From Montreal, the Services travelled to Toronto and stayed there for a couple of days, then visited with Robert's brother Stanley and his family in Ottawa. The Services then continued by train to Jasper, Alberta, where they relaxed in a log cabin, walked around Lake Beauvert, and toured Maligne Canyon.

In September 1940, while the Services were still in Jasper, the real Sam McGee died in Beiseker, Alberta. Once the media heard about McGee's death, they bombarded Robert with questions. Robert commented that Sam McGee had been "a very fine type of sourdough prospector."

The real Sam McGee was born in Ontario in 1867 to Irish parents. He went to the Yukon in 1898 in search of gold. Though he didn't find any, he did make a fortune as a builder of cabins and bridges. After living for a time in Montana, where he built the highway to Yellowstone Park, he moved to Beiseker, and is now buried there, in Levelland Cemetery.

It was while he lived in Whitehorse that Robert had come across McGee's name in the bank ledger and had thought it would fit well into his new verse. When he'd asked McGee if he could use his name, McGee had said, "Go ahead." But after the poem had become famous and people were laughing, McGee hadn't been impressed, so he'd decided to get even.

One afternoon, Robert had wanted to go over some wild rapids just for the experience, and had climbed aboard McGee's canoe just as it was leaving the shore. Once the boat had reached mid-stream, McGee turned to Robert and said, "You cremated me once. I think I'll drown you now." He had then proceeded to take him on an exhilarating and unforgettable wild ride over the rapids. When it was over, a laughing McGee had said, "There, I got you back."

The *Cremation of Sam McGee* had brought different kinds of world fame to both men, and it seemed fitting that Robert should attend McGee's funeral. Reports say he arrived late and slipped quietly into the back during the funeral service, having first gone to the wrong church.

The Services arrived in Vancouver on October 20, 1940. Media continued to seek out the 66-year-old poet for interviews and photographs. Indeed, the return of Vancouver's famous former resident was big news. The family rented Tudor Manor on Sylvia Court and settled in for the next few months. Robert took plea-sure in reuniting with his sister Agnes and brother Peter (who now owned the Sourdough Bookshop on Vancouver's West Pender Street).

Robert was enjoying his time in Canada, but he never went back to visit Yukon he had left 38 years earlier. (Some stories have surfaced saying that in August 1940, he did fly to the Yukon with Southern Air Transport, but most researchers say he did not.) In Vancouver, he openly voiced his opinions about the Sec-ond World War and discussed how he missed being in France. "I

The real Sam McGee and his wife, Ruth Warnes,
in Peterborogh, Ontario, June 5, 1901.
PHOTO COURTESY OF BEVERLY GRAMMS

Sam McGee in 1938, just before he travelled to New York
for an interview on the NBC program We the People.
PHOTO COURTESY OF BEVERLY GRAMMS

feel almost as if I am shirking something. After living for a year
in the war zone you get used to the atmosphere. Every moment
is exciting."

He longed to be either back in France or in sunny California.
So, after spending Christmas in Vancouver with his relatives, Robert and his family headed to Hollywood.

Robert Service with his wife Germaine (right) and his
daughter Iris (left), in Canada during the war years.
LAC PA-178390

California Calls ... Again

For the next five years, the Services maintained dual residences;
they wintered in Hollywood and returned every spring to Vancouver. Meanwhile, the press continued to seek Robert out. At one
point he told reporters, "It seems as if [the Yukon ballads were]
written by another man. I remember little of the Yukon, or what
I wrote there."

When asked what his advice was to emerging poets, he said,
"Write verse, not poetry. The public wants verse. If you have a talent

for poetry, then don't try by any means to smother it, but try your hand in verse."

Robert continued to tackle new projects. He did his first radio broadcast on October 18, 1941, for Vancouver's CKWX, and he delivered his first public speech on November 12 to the Hollywood Author's Society.

When Pearl Harbour was attacked in December, bringing the United States into the Second World War, Robert was in California and immediately joined the war effort. For five months, he travelled through the southwestern United States, touring army camps, performing at USO concerts, and talking to the troops. Whenever he recited *The Shooting of Dan McGrew* or *The Cremation of Sam McGee*, there was thunderous applause.

Always ready for a new adventure, Robert then became a Hollywood movie star. It all started when Frank Lloyd (who produced the 1928 film adaptation of Robert's book *The Pretender*) asked Robert if he would play himself in the film *The Spoilers*. It was a story about the Alaska gold rush from a book written by Rex Beach. The leading stars would include Marlene Dietrich, Randolph Scott, and John Wayne.

Robert only had twenty-seven words to speak in the movie, but he practised them intensely. He even hired a drama coach, who told him not to make any gestures and to keep his face expressionless. The outfit he chose for his movie role as himself made him look like a cross between a miner, a cowboy, a roughneck, and Billy the Kid. Makeup artist Jack Pierce made Robert look thirty-seven years younger, using as reference a tintype photograph taken of him when he was a bank clerk in Whitehorse.

Robert Service and Marlene Dietrich on the set of *The Spoilers*.
UNIVERSAL STUDIOS

Working with Marlene Dietrich was a big thrill for Robert. He later wrote of the experience, "Then from behind me a vision of sizzling beauty, the divine Dietrich. She wore a gown of gold, and as she looked at me her ice-blue eyes thrilled me to my marrow." *The Spoilers*, the only movie that Robert ever appeared in, premiered on May 21, 1942, and received good reviews.

By the end of October 1943, Robert had started another monumental work: the first book of his autobiography, *Ploughman of the Moon*. A year later, he was finished and sent the 150,000-word manuscript to his publisher, Frank Dodd. He later wrote, "During the whole year I worked hard on my book. It was tough going at first, for the drag-nets of memory did not prove too rich in glittering trove. I toiled valiantly, however, and pictures of the remotest past came to reward me... From the murk and gloom scenes vivid and vital projected themselves, and triumphantly I pounced on them. Bit by bit I filled in the frame of my tapestry, thinking, what a marvellous thing is visual memory! How was it I could reconstruct an event of sixty years ago as if it were yesterday? Yet, there it was, incredible as a photograph, preserved by some magical process of the mind." Memories of his father were particularly meaningful to him and he dedicated the book, "To the Memory of My Father," adding a couplet:

> *Full of rich earthiness, a Grand Old Guy,*
> *With all his faults a better man than I.*

Ploughman of the Moon was published in the fall of 1945 and received mixed reviews. One newspaper reviewer, Stanley Walker, dismissed it as "not a very good book," saying Service "over-writes his tales dreadfully," and calling him the "world's most assiduous user of cliches." Walker did acknowledge, though, that Robert had become "the singer of the Common Man."

Even as an autobiographer, Robert remained the storyteller extraordinaire, embellishing stories, omitting dates, changing names, and adding imaginative details and people to move the story along. Future biographers would find it a challenge to sort out the storytelling from the non-fiction.

As Geoffrey T. Heilman of the *New Yorker* observed in 1945, "[Robert Service] concentrates on moods and impressions rather than on names, facts and figures. Thus a reader of the autobiography might easily suppose that he was perusing the vague memoirs of a literary vagabond… rather than those of an author whose ballads have netted him a substantial fortune and have for nearly forty years been as familiar as Shakespeare to millions of people."

The popular press and the public liked the book, and *Ploughman of the Moon* became a bestseller.

Going Home to France

With the war over, Robert and his family left Hollywood in December 1945, and headed for New York. Robert pulled some strings with senior executives of American Express to get passage across the Atlantic on the *Bardstown Victory*, a troopship bound for Marseilles.

At that time, he was almost seventy-two years old, a famous and wealthy poet who had lived for the past fifty years on his royalties. But Robert's most prolific writing was yet to come. In

114

the last nine years of his life—between the ages of seventy-seven and eighty-four—Robert would write more poetry than he had ever written before. Starting with *Songs of a Sun Lover* in 1949, he would publish eight new volumes of work before his death in 1958.

CHAPTER

8

The Last
Years

THE SS *BARDSTOWN Victory* had just returned to New York, bringing home 1500 American soldiers from Europe. Now, as it headed
back across the Atlantic to pick up more soldiers, the ship was virtu-
ally empty. It carried only fifteen civilian passengers, including the
Services. The weather was bitterly cold and there was a fierce gale
blowing—winter crossings on the Atlantic were seldom pleasant.

The Services were in a four-berth cabin that had served as the
isolation unit of the ship's hospital. Their cabin turned from icebox
to oven once the ship's heat was turned on. To keep cool at night,
Robert opened the cabin door wide, but then they had to listen to
the racket of the engines. Getting to sleep was difficult.

Things got worse: Robert developed influenza, took to bed, and
simply read. It was cold but sunny when they docked at Marseilles.

Later, at the train station in Nice, a weak and coughing Robert stumbled on the platform, hurting his hip.

In the summer of 1946, the Services didn't return to summer at Dream Haven, as had been their pre-war routine. Instead, they moved to Monte Carlo and rented two floors of the Villa Aurora, near the northern end of Monte Carlo. This would be their winter home for the next twelve years. He called it Sourdough Hall, as the ongoing royalties from his early ballads paid for the rent.

In his seventies now, Robert was still a handsome-looking man, trim figured in his dark shorts, sandals, and beret. In mid-summer of 1947, he finished the second volume of his autobiography, *Harper of Heaven*, and it was published the following year. He had wanted to name the book *Blue-behinded Ape* in reference to Robert Louis Stevenson's poem "Portrait," but was talked out of it. Instead, he took the name *Harper of Heaven* from the quatrain he inserted on the title page:

> *Although my sum of years may*
> *Nigh seventy and seven*
> *With eyes of ecstasy I see*
> *And hear the Harps of Heaven.*

The book received worldwide attention. Some critics called it a tough, violent book, while others said it was "one of the most inspirational."

Post-War Dream Haven

Although the Service's Nice apartment had not been destroyed during the war, it was a different scene at Dream Haven. The

Germans had stripped everything of value, and had looted the house. Robert's grand piano had been shipped to Hamburg. His motorbike and prized collection of guitars had vanished.

The family soon learned that during the war, Dream Haven had been home to a Germany infantry platoon. Later, the house had been fortified, with pillboxes erected in the garden, a network of trenches and tunnels dug, and concrete platforms installed for gun emplacements. In Robert's library, the fine bindings, rare editions, and reference books had disappeared. Only a third of his library books remained, and they were all damaged beyond repair.

The 73-year-old Robert was determined to restore Dream Haven, and though it took him a few summers, he did complete the refurbishment.

Last Trip to Canada

Robert was a bit undecided about what to do next, when fate gave him one last opportunity to return to Canada. In 1948, the International Sourdough's Association was holding its fiftieth anniversary celebration of the Trail of the Ninety-Eight from August 12 to 14 in Vancouver. Assuming he would not be able to attend the celebration in person, the association sent Robert a telegram asking if he could send them a congratulatory cable to read to the participants. He surprised them when he replied, "In spirit be damned. Why not in the ruddy flesh?"

The convention organizers were delighted! At seventy-four years of age, and with his family in tow, Robert travelled the 11,000-kilometre journey one more time, crossing the Atlantic by ship and Canada by rail to Vancouver. The trip exhausted him.

He delivered a magnificent, emotional speech at the convention: "All the things I am and have, I owe to the North. That far-off cold and silent land has made better men of all who have ever come out of it." When asked if he planned to return to Yukon, he replied that he didn't have the time to go back. "There's no time for anything but work."

On September 4, 1948, the family boarded the Canadian Pacific liner *Empress of Canada* in Montreal, bound for Liverpool. Robert would not return to Canada again.

Back home in Monte Carlo, he had work to do and no time to waste. The next year, 1949, he published *Songs of a Sun Lover*, and a year later, *Rhymes of a Roughneck*. *Lyrics of a Lowbrow* (1951) took a nostalgic look back at the Klondike days, at the dance halls, girls, and gambling saloons. There was now a sense of urgency in his poems. In *Envoi*, he asks for time:

O *God! Please let me write*
Just one book more.

His prayer in verse was answered. *Rhymes of a Rebel* was published in 1952, followed by *Songs for My Supper* (1953), *Carols of an Old Codger* (1954), and *Rhymes for My Rags* (1956).

Six years before Robert died, his daughter Iris (then 35) married James Llewellyn Davis, a former Royal Air Force lieutenant of the First World War and now the manager of the Monte Carlo branch of the Lloyd's bank. Robert's first granddaughter, Anne, was born in 1952, and two years later, a second granddaughter, Armelle, was born.

The aging poet still had a free spirit that hungered for travel. He said he wanted to visit Australia, New Zealand, and South America before he died. He added, "I would also have liked to visit China but I'm afraid I've left that too late." He never made it to any of those destinations.

Now in his eighties, Robert continued to prolifically create verse. When he was eighty-two years old and living in Monte Carlo, the famous movie star Grace Kelly married Monaco's Prince Rainer III. Robert's wedding present to Princess Grace was a leather-bound edition of his collected works. Inscribed on the flyleaf was an illuminated manuscript of a poem dedicated to Grace Kelly, simply entitled "To G.K." Newspapers now hailed him as the Poet Laureate of Monaco.

One of the reporters covering the royal wedding went to interview Robert at his home. He found a "short gentleman with a French wife, a ruddy face, a fuzz of grey hair, and the remains of a Scottish accent."

Robert told him, "I am just a writer of verse. I write every morning. Sometimes I manage three poems in a day. I build up a stock, then I make a selection and publish a volume." His plan for longevity was a special program of diet and exercise. "I eat no breakfast, a light lunch with very little meat, a good evening meal which usually consists of rice, porridge and potatoes. I walk hard for three hours every day and I have a daily swim for six months of the year."

By the mid 1950s, Robert's first book of verse, *Songs of a Sourdough*, had sold 3 million copies, and the volumes of his original Yukon ballads had never been out of print. He told the reporter,

"Nobody writes about me these days, but somebody must read the books, because they go on selling."

In August 1958, Robert caught influenza and was confined to bed for several weeks. Iris and her family came to Dream Haven to visit with him. Then, on September 11, 1958, Robert went for a short morning stroll along the water, had a light lunch, and, as was his routine, went to bed afterwards. Later that afternoon with Germaine by his side, he died.

The Final Goodbye

Robert had wanted to be buried at Lancieux. A few days after his death, a simple funeral was held, attended by relatives from Britain and Canada. A horse-drawn hearse passed slowly down the street that bore his name. At the bistro along the way, the hearse halted and, as was the local custom, the coachman went inside for a refreshment before continuing to the cemetery.

Robert's gravesite lies at the centre of the cemetery at Lancieux. Inscribed in gold letters on the headstone is ROBERT SERVICE 1874–1958.

Germaine Service died in Monte Carlo on December 26, 1989, at the age of 102. Robert's daughter Iris continues to live in Monte Carlo, and his grand-daughter Anne, in France. Granddaughter Armelle lived in New Zealand and died in 1996.

Epilogue

ROBERT SERVICE'S VERSE and prose spoke to everyone, regardless of one's education, nationality, or occupation. His fans ran the gamut from royalty (such as Queen Marie of Romania, Prince Philip, and the late Queen Mother) to presidents, politicians, nurses, pilots, and young students. Charles Lindberg took along a book of Service's poems when he made his historic flight across the Atlantic Ocean.

Robert always insisted that he was a rhymer and a versifier, not a poet. Many disagree, calling him a great poet, as did the *Pittsburgh Sun Telegraph* in an obituary they published after his death: "A great poet died last week in Lancieux, France, at the age of 84. He was not a poet's poet. Fancy-Dan dilettantes will dispute the description 'great.' He was a people's poet. To the people, he was great. They understood him, and knew that any verse carrying the by-line of Robert W. Service would be a lilting thing, clear, clean and power-packed, beating out a story with a dramatic intensity that made the nerves tingle."

Bibliography

Berton, Pierre. *Klondike: The Last Great Gold Rush, 1896–1899*. Toronto: McClelland & Stewart, 1997.

Klinck, Carl F. *Robert Service: A Biography*. New York: Dodd, Mead & Company, 1976.

Lockhart, G.W. *On The Trail of Robert Service*. Edinburgh: Luath Press Limited, 1999.

MacKay, James. *Vagabond of Verse*. Edinburgh: Mainstream, 1995.

Madame Anne Longépé. Personal Correspondence.

Service, Robert. *Harper of Heaven: A Record of Radiant Living*. New York: Dodd, Mead & Company, 1948.

———. *Ploughman of the Moon: An Adventure Into Memory*. New York: Dodd, Mead & Company, 1945.

———. *Rhymes of a Rolling Stone*. Toronto, William Briggs, 1912.

———. *Songs of a Sourdough*. Toronto: William Briggs, 1907

Stevenson, Robert Louis. *The Amateur Emigrant*. London: Hogarth Press, 1984.

Wetherell, Donald G. and Irene R.A. Kmet. *Alberta's North: A History 1890–1950*. Edmonton: Canadian Circumpolar Institute Press and Alberta Community Development, 2000.

Yukon Tourism, Heritage Branch. *Overland Trail: Whitehorse-Dawson*. 1998.

Acknowledgments

RESEARCHING AND WRITING a book connects an author to people with various expertise: archivists, academics, historians, other writers, librarians, individuals linked to the subject by kin or circumstance, and many more. In writing this biography on Robert Service, I was networked with many people who were generous in answering questions and providing me with resources and detail.

Special acknowledgements go out to Heather Jones at the Yukon Archives; Anne Morton at the Hudson's Bay Company Archives; Dr. Tory Tronrud at the Thunder Bay Museum; and the Reference Section of Thunder Bay Public Library. Your expertise and assistance is much appreciated.

Thank you also to those individuals who provided valuable assistance, like Wayne Ducher, who kindly shared his family's private collection of estate journals, diaries, and photos from the 1911–1912 Douglas Expedition; journalist and researcher Peter Mitham, for access to his research and published/unpublished articles on Robert Service; Doug Bell, who proofread the text; and Dr. Mike Gismondi at Athabasca University, for directing me to resources regarding the Athabasca.

Acknowledgements and heartfelt appreciation also go to my family for their continuing support. Special thanks to my daughter Tania for reviewing my manuscript draft and offering excellent suggestions; to my daughters Cindi and Tami for always being enthusiastic about my writings; and to my husband Glenn for his understanding and sense of humour, even as the growing stacks of research material spread from my office to the rest of the house.

I would also like to acknowledge Kara Turner (of my original publisher, Altitude Publishing), for providing me with the opportunity to author the book on Robert Service; to editor Jill Foran, for her professionalism and positive approach in editing the book; and, to the production and marketing teams that brought the biography to print and to the book market.

In his memoirs, Robert Service commented on writing a record of his life: "Let the biographer chronicle them, when one is dead." I acknowledge and applaud him for writing two autobiographies that challenge his biographers to also become historical detectives.

Index

Index

Index

Index

About
the Author

ELLE ANDRA-WARNER IS a long-time resident of Thunder Bay, but has recently also
lived in Alberta and the Northwest Territories. Estonian by heritage, she was born in a
post-war Estonian displaced persons camp
in Europe, and came to Canada as a child
with her parents.

A graduate of Lakehead University, she specializes in non-fiction
writing, focussing on history, biographies, aviation, and travel destinations. Her weekly newspaper column about people is in its tenth
year of publication, and her feature articles appear in publications
around the world.